# IMAGES
## OF
# POWER

*HOW THE IMAGE MAKERS*
*SHAPE OUR LEADERS*

## BRENDAN BRUCE

KOGAN
PAGE

First published in 1992

Kogan Page Limited
120 Pentonville Road
London N1 9JN

**British Library Cataloguing in Publication Data**

A CIP record for this book is available from the British Library.
ISBN 0 7494 0669 0

Typeset by Saxon Printing Ltd, Derby
Printed and bound in Great Britain by Biddles Ltd, Guildford and Kings Lynn

# Contents

Preface                                             5

*Chapter 1* – On the Shoulders of Giants            9

*Chapter 2* – First Impressions                    39

*Chapter 3* – The Marketing of Power               81

*Chapter 4* – Managing the News                   127

Epilogue                                          177

Selected Bibliography                             183

Index                                             184

*For Dominic and Mary Bruce*

# Preface

This book is about how leaders and their image makers create the images that make them successful and powerful. There are many reasons for writing a comprehensive analysis of this subject (the most obvious being that no image maker has ever written one before), but the most compelling is that three basic, but important, questions continually go unanswered. What exactly is image making? How important is it in the process whereby those who wish to govern us gain the power to do so? Is it a good or a bad influence on our lives?

Until now the image makers themselves have mostly kept silent about their work, remaining largely unknown outside a small circle of insiders and experts in government, business and the media. In 1968 a young reporter called Joe McGinnis gained access to the Nixon election campaign team and wrote a best-selling account of image makers at work. The media's interest in the subject was greatly increased by the Conservative party's appointment of Saatchi & Saatchi in the late 1970s. Since the 1979 election several key figures have emerged from the shadows. The contribution of Gordon Reece and Tim Bell (both subsequently knighted) to Margaret Thatcher's success has been widely recognised, and Sir Bernard Ingham became the first chief press secretary at No 10 to become a household name.

The growing awareness of the importance of image making in the election of leaders and the activities of business and government, has been accompanied by a parallel increase in interest shown by the general public in image making as an influence in their personal lives. Since the 1960s there has been a growing feeling that one is not predestined to be either unfit, ugly, overweight, badly educated, ill-informed or stuck in the social class into which one's parents were born. A whole industry has grown up, of which Samuel Smiles would be proud, to teach people what most schools don't, ie how to present themselves effectively through improving their appearance and increasing their self-confidence. People have learnt about 'style' and 'taste' in ways previously confined to, and jealously guarded by, the middle classes. They now have access to detailed information about diet, exercise, make-up, food, foreign travel, clothes, décor and so on, which simply didn't exist 40 years ago.

Life-skills education is now widespread. Women learn about post-family retraining, assertiveness and how to protect themselves – giving them the self-confidence to face men as equals. Budding tycoons of both sexes learn about starting their own business; leadership and communication skills; time management and decision making. All this has made the public conscious that something called 'image' exists and that it is a powerful force in late 20th-century life.

Much of what little there is to read about the subject is, however, consistently shallow – if not downright misleading. Some journalists take the trouble to master the subject, but most tack between relentless trivialization and breathtaking ignorance of its history. Many have no idea, for example, where the techniques of image making come from or the enormous influence of Hollywood. The difference between the three key disciplines of personal image, marketing and news management is only dimly understood. None of which is any help to the interested observer of current events who wants to understand the subject, assess its importance and decide whether it is a legitimate weapon of leadership.

This book is an attempt to help the reader understand an important part of the world they live in, so that they may be equipped to shape it to their own vision. The principal object of government should be to protect individual freedom and it is vital that the free citizen understands how the state and its leaders operate. If, having gained this knowledge, they allow the leviathan to swallow them whole rather than protect their freedoms, that is their choice. It should not be a course of action based on simple ignorance.

*Preface*

It would not be possible to write such a book without the advice, encouragement and help of many colleagues and friends. I owe a special debt of gratitude to the following:

Sir Tom Arnold MP; Jeffrey Archer; The Right Honourable Kenneth Baker PC, MP; Ray Barker; Sir Tim Bell; Drayton Bird; Adam Boulton; Michael Bruce; Michael Brunson; Lord Callaghan of Cardiff; Alastair Campbell; Philippa Davies; Barry Delaney; John Desborough CBE; Michael Dobbs; Gary Duckworth; Winston Fletcher; Sally Ford-Hutchinson; Gennadi Gerasimov; Fiona Gilmore; Ian Greer; Peter Gummer; Tony Hall; John Hanvey CBE; John Hegarty; Sir Bernard Ingham; Howell James; Michael Jones; George Jones; Professor Dennis Kavanagh; Tony Kerpel MBE; Philip Kurland; Sir Christopher Lawson; Peter Mandelson; Gus O'Donnell; Stewart Purvis; John Salmon; Michael Shea CVO; Mary Spillane; Iain Sproat; Gary Strachan; Harvey Thomas CBE; John Underwood; Michael White; John Whittingdale OBE; Robin Wight; Dr Richard Wirthlin and Lord Young of Graffham, together with all those who preferred to give their help anonymously.

Thanks also go to my research assistant Luca Carloni and to Philip Mudd of Kogan Page.

*Brendan Bruce*
*St Eutrope de Born*
*and Belgravia*
*January 1992*

# 1

# On the Shoulders of Giants

*If I have seen further, it is by standing on the shoulders of giants.*

Sir Isaac Newton

## Early days

On the morning of 23 August 1485, Henry Tudor awoke, king of England. The preceding day he had convincingly defeated Richard III at Bosworth Field, yet his claim to the throne rested on a dubious connection through his mother. Henry set about legitimizing his position in a characteristically energetic and efficient way.

First, he married Elizabeth of York, Richard's niece, thus merging the two warring factions of Lancaster and York. Secondly, he did what any corporate design expert would advise in a contested merger and combined the symbols of the two houses, the red and white roses respectively, creating what we know as the 'Tudor Rose' and had it featured on royal buildings, clothes and documents. He then set out to blacken his predecessor's name, even going to the extent of ordering changes to Richard's portrait to make him look like a hunchback – a process of vilification later continued by Shakespeare, who repeated Sir Thomas More's calumny that Richard murdered the 'Princes in the Tower'. Lastly, he (despite his miserly nature) quite deliberately embarked on a campaign to convey an impression of

[9]

power, prestige and wealth through his portraits by Maynard Werwick.

What we would today call the Tudor corporate image was designed by stonemasons, tailors, manuscript illuminators, poets, painters and court historians. It was a highly successful campaign. By his death in 1509, the Yorkist cause was forgotten and Richard's reputation was blackened so effectively that it is only now that we are learning the truth. The Tudor dynasty had been both legitimized and firmly established.

Henry Tudor's son Henry VIII encountered the same image problem of legitimacy, but in an entirely different and potentially more dangerous way. In 1533, Henry declared that 'England was a sovereign state and its King owed no submission to any other human ruler'. He was now head of the Church in England and no longer considered that his authority came from the Pope, but from God direct.

Like all image makers, his two advisers – Thomas Cromwell and Hans Holbein the Younger – took advantage of new technology. Cromwell started by producing a series of laws designed to reduce the authority of the clergy and increase the king's power to rule by proclamation. Holbein's stunning portrait of 1536 stared down all those who dared to question. His massive torso (he was 6 ft 2 inches tall) is covered in gold, rubies, pearls, fur and velvet. Henry looks coldly at us, with his clear blue eyes having no pretence of approachability. His lips are pursed in contempt for the world and its uncooperative bishops of Rome. He has just ordered Anne Boleyn's head to be chopped off, but there is no sign of anguish or remorse.

This aggressive, egotistical image of raw power was reproduced for the masses by the new technology of wood-cut printing, on the coins of the period by Bruschal and in the first mass communications campaign of modern times – the Great Bible. Cromwell persuaded his boss that a vernacular bible was desirable and in 1539 this volume was produced on the recently invented printing press and distributed to every parish church throughout the kingdom – complete with its title page showing Henry distributing the 'verbum dei' to his grateful subjects while its author looks on.

   The story of the house of Tudor has all the ingredients of any
successful takeover campaign: a simple problem; a clear strategy; expert advisers who understand the new technology; and
ruthless destruction of the opposition. Image making today may
be more complex in form, but it is scarcely more sophisticated or
successful. As G R Elton has observed, there is no king of
England who is more familiar than Henry VIII and his is still the
only portrait which is recognized instantly by the vast majority of
his successor's subjects. Films, plays and books continue to be
written about him and his daughter Elizabeth 400 years on – not
bad for a family business that lasted for only 118 years.

## Facts, facts, facts – the power of the press

Lord Northcliffe said, 'God made the people read so that I could
fill their brains with facts, facts, facts – and later tell them whom
to love, whom to hate, and what to think' and for 300 years the
powerful looked to newspapers to spread their ideas, describe
their triumphs, enumerate their finer points and generally keep
the population in a permanent state of awe and gratitude for
their very existence. For 300 years journalists have had other
ideas. When I say 'newspapers' they were nothing like – in form
or content – what 20th-century readers would recognize as such.
   The modern concept of a newspaper is no older than the
beginning of modern democracy, that is the 1830s. Nothing
better illustrates my thesis that image making is driven by a
combination of technological development and the widening of
the franchise than the growth of newspapers. Without an
increase in the numbers eligible to vote, the powerful did not
need a mass circulation medium. Without printing presses
capable of printing thousands of copies per hour, and a fast
distribution system, all these new voters could not be reached.
Without a growth in literacy and the ability to pay for these
products, there was no market for them.
   Science and the Whigs were, however, at hand. The latter
forced through the 1832 Reform Act which widened the
franchise by 80 per cent. Science provided in the steam engine a
fast, inexpensive distribution system to send the newspapers to
every town in the country, not in a matter of days, as the coach

[11]

mails had taken, but in hours. The Whigs responded in 1836 by lowering the duty payable on newspapers by 75 per cent, from fourpence to a penny. Science trumped this with the invention of the telegraph in 1837, which made the gathering of news from all over the country easy and quick. When the telegraph cable was laid across the Atlantic in 1860 the British voter could even read about great events in the US. American readers read accounts in their morning paper of battles that had taken place the day before, with the bodies still lying on the field.

Mr Hoe gave us in 1846 the rotary press – capable of a staggering 20,000 copies per hour by printing on a continuous sheet of paper and on both sides. Not to be outdone, British politicians abolished the duty on advertisements, encouraging business to use the medium, thus funding even more technological developments. The government, with a flourish, then abolished the duty on newspapers altogether. Familiar names began to appear; the *News of the World* and the *Daily Telegraph*. The Associated Press and the Press Association were founded.

The politicians responded again, this time by doubling the numbers of those eligible to vote in the 1867 Reform Act and more importantly increasing the literacy rate, when in the 1870 Education Act they made it compulsory for every child to be taught to read.

A new kind of journalist appeared at political events, the agency reporter. On 19 November 1863, President Lincoln spoke for a few minutes at the dedication of a cemetery in Pennsylvania. His words not being considered particularly newsworthy on that sad occasion, little note of what he said was taken, although one newspaper did record 'the President also spoke'. The only reason we know what he did say is that an AP reporter asked him for his notes. The cemetery was at Gettysburg.

There was even an AP reporter at Little Big Horn. He never filed his report as Crazy Horse got to him first.

Both North and South used a new breed of journalist during the American Civil War – the PR writer. These writers were paid to write articles mainly for English newspapers, to tour Britain making speeches and to bribe journalists to plant favourable news items and editorials. Newspaper editors started to be courted by the powerful. J T Delane of *The Times* was a close confidant of both Aberdeen and Palmerston and has been described as an 'honorary non-voting member of the House of Commons'. A new and compelling feature idea was developed; 'the interview'. The first interview with a public figure took place in Salt Lake City, Utah, when Horace Greeley of the *New York Tribune* interviewed the Mormon leader, Brigham Young.

## The rise of the investigative reporter

What really revolutionized the power élite's view of journalists however, was the reporting of the Crimean War. *The Times* decided to send William Howard Russell to the peninsula to write the usual dispatches describing military movements and strategy. Instead, he filed a dramatic series of reports (sent by the telegraph) about the conditions the troops were enduring both on the march and in the dreadful, disease-ridden 'hospitals' that Florence Nightingale was determined to reform. He also pursued the military high command and its staff with a manic vengeance, deliberately trying to bring Raglan down.

The government's first reaction in re-introducing the press censorship that had been abandoned in 1693, was quickly overtaken when the public demanded Russell's reports continue. The press had successfully flexed its muscles for the first time.

Investigative reporting spread to social issues. In London, W T Stead's peppery sermons boomed out from his pulpit at the *Pall Mall Gazette*. He set out to whip up public indignation at the ghastly London slums, attacking both church and Parliament for doing nothing, until the government was forced to establish a Royal Commission.

He then turned his guns on the issue of the age of consent for girls, which was 13 at that time. After the Commons had refused to back the Lords in passing legislation to prevent young girls being sold to brothels, Stead set about interviewing procurers, pimps, prostitutes, social workers and policemen to gather evidence. To test the system he bought a young virgin called Eliza Armstrong for £5 (complete with midwife's attestation of virginity and chloroform to enable her to be broken in by gang rape) and handed her over to the Salvation Army.

Stead was a first-class tabloid journalist and knew exactly how to use the new multi-decker headline layout, with cross-heads

[13]

and illustrations, to manipulate public opinion. His reports were emblazoned with such classic heads as 'I order Five Virgins' and 'The Confessions of a London Brothel-Keeper'. The government was furious and, dragooned into raising the age of consent to 15, it took its revenge against Stead by charging him with the abduction of little Eliza. Found guilty and sentenced to three months' imprisonment, he became martyr and hero, mere journalist no longer, yet the tradition had taken hold and the notion that newspapers not only recorded but actually made news was born.

From this point on, the powerful veered between a desire to shoot journalists down like dogs and fawning over them in the hope that their reviews would be flattering (in my observation, both often being done in the course of a few minutes). Politicians, being mostly practical creatures when it comes to overcoming opposition, soon found a pragmatic and non-violent middle way. After initially banning them from the Members' Lobby, a small, enclosed area just outside the chamber of the Commons, the Speaker instituted in 1885 what was called a 'lobby list', to allow selected daily journalists to stand (only members have a right to sit) in the lobby and catch members as they walked between the chamber and the rest of the Palace of Westminster.

At first resented and rebuffed – when they weren't being ignored – the privileged few gradually asserted their 'rights' to ask ministers and members their opinions about the issues of the day. As the politicians realized that their promised anonymity was indeed kept, they started to use the lobby correspondents as a proxy for attacks on their colleagues (the real enemy for any professional politician), digs at the official opposition, resentment of the whips' office (*plus ça change*) and puffs for themselves. The reporters covered the debates, while the grandee editors mixed socially with cabinet ministers and retailed their more elevated views in the leader columns.

### The birth of the tabloid

After the 1867 Reform Act, the political parties were rapidly organizing to communicate with the new voters, because as Lord Derby (then foreign secretary) said in 1875, the working man 'can, if he chooses, outvote all other classes put together'. New types of magazines were started to cater for this popular audience. First *Tit-Bits* and then *Answers*, which satisfied the people's insatiable curiosity for such trivial but fascinating facts as Queen Victoria's height (4 ft 10 in) and the colour of Mr Gladstone's socks (red). *Answers* was the brainchild of a 23-year-old journalist who went on to revolutionize the newspaper business on 4 May 1896 when his new popular newspaper called the *Daily Mail* went on sale for the first time (as did tickets for the first film show).

Alfred Charles Harmsworth, 1st (and only) Viscount Northcliffe, was an Irishman whose fascination with any manifestation of the *zeitgeist*, and ability to predict exactly which of them would attract his readers, made him the creator of modern popular journalism. Helped by his brother Harold (the future Lord Rothermere), he became interested in the idea of a paper that the lower-middle class could understand and afford; ('written for office boys, by office boys' said Salisbury); a paper that would cover the news briefly and in plain English; have no party affiliation to undermine its independent stance; and have modern features such as a woman's page, and which would feature crime but no sex. All this for a ha'penny. Within four years the *Mail* was selling nearly a million copies. Respectable clerks read it on the train going to their offices, and advertising money poured in. The business (which went public in 1905) boomed, allowing Northcliffe to buy *The Times,* the *Observer,* the *Daily Mirror,* the *Evening News,* plus a string of provincial newspapers. In all, about half the nation read a Northcliffe paper every day.

Northcliffe became so powerful that when he decided to hound Lord Chancellor Haldane out of office for suspected pro-German leanings, not only did he succeed, but not one voice in the cabinet was raised in Haldane's defence. After war broke out Lloyd George effectively silenced Northcliffe (who refused a cabinet seat) by appointing him head of the British War Mission in the US and subsequently head of the government's propaganda effort. Never again would politicians allow anyone to be so powerful that their power would eclipse that of the political establishment, so when, much later, Beaverbrook arrived at the zenith of his powers, Baldwin was ready for him.

The flow of Victorian inventiveness had continued unabated throughout the last third of the century, the typewriter (1874), the telephone (1876), paper from wood pulp (1880), linotype (1890) and radio (1891) all increasing the speed and ease of communications and each one widening the image makers' scope to increase the hold on power of political and business leaders. The invention that was to have the biggest effect on newspapers' ability to create images was the development of dry plate photography in 1873 and the half-tone block process which allowed photographs to be reproduced in newspapers for the first time.

## Relating to the public

By the end of the 19th century the power of newspapers was causing anxiety among industrialists on both sides of the Atlantic. In the half century following the US Civil War and before the outbreak of the Great War, a few men had accumulated power and fortunes of incredible size. Between 1892 and 1899, Rockefeller's personal dividends from Standard Oil amounted to nearly $50 million, and in 1900 alone Andrew Carnegie's income from his steel interests amounted to $23 million. These 'robber barons', and those who lived off the income they generated, caused violent publicity storms. When the growing power of trade unions disrupted production, the barons produced a new weapon to beat the strikers – the PR man.

The 'barons' had used press agents from the start to get favourable coverage – they even managed to cover up their role in the 1869 Black Friday panic when thousands were ruined. When in 1906 the Pennsylvania Railroad Company experienced a bad train accident they brought in a new breed of PR man, Ivy L Lee. Lee's philosophy was based on openness, which up to then had been anathema to industry bosses. He reversed the usual news blackout and invited reporters to travel at the railroad's expense to the scene of the crash. Facilities were set up for them to write their stories and take photographs. The Pennsylvania, which had traditionally endured a bad press, got one of the best presses it ever had. Lee was soon hired by John D Rockefeller II himself, for $1000 a month, to smooth over the effects of the

'Ludlow Massacre', when Rockefeller's Colorado Fuel and Iron Co decided to settle the strike by shooting the workforce.

The phrase 'public relations' was invented by Edward L Bernays (Freud's nephew and deeply influenced by psychological theory) who, after Lee, has a claim to be the first 20th-century PR 'counsel', rather than the Victorian 'press agent'. Bernays dealt in solutions to problems – how to increase a magazine's circulation or sales of bacon, helping a hair-net company stem the vogue for 'bobbed' hair (by making it socially unacceptable), the Lithuanian people gain independence or New York City shuck off its image as 'cold and inhospitable'. Bernays' favourite solution was what he called 'creating events', eg awards, surveys and contests, a common enough technique now, but revolutionary in its day. Bernays talked about 'societal technicians' and 'engineering consent' (starting the PR industry's fondness for neologisms) in opposing industry's previous attitude of 'the public be damned'. He argued that the public had the right to be informed and have its questions answered promptly and fairly. He claimed that his clients had an equal right to press their case, so long as deception was not involved.

## Radio days

The first medium to challenge newspapers' hegemony over communications was the radio. As Dr H H Crippen said, 'What a marvellous invention it is! How privileged we are to be alive in an age of such scientific miracles', but this challenge was an unusually slow process for, while Edison patented the radio in 1891, (and the first broadcast took place exactly ten years later) it took until 1920 for regular broadcasts to start in America – 1923 in Britain. In 1919 a handful of listeners listened for the first time as their president spoke. By 1922, 220 stations were established, and the $10 radio was selling by the million.

Unsurprisingly perhaps, politicians fell in love with the new medium. Harding equipped his campaign train with a radio transmitter when he realized that stump speaking was a thing of the past. Radio's reach was unimaginably greater than 19th-century politicians could dream of: in 1896 William Jennings Bryan had reached 5 million voters by travelling 18,000 miles in

27 states; F D Roosevelt could reach 60 million without leaving his office. With impressive speed, politicians and their advisers learnt that radio was a conversational not a declamatory medium, unsuited to Victorian voice projection. They also learnt that the early microphones were limited in their ability to pick up speech, so they could not move away from it or turn to address people standing behind them (a lesson still to be learnt by some current members of the House of Commons!).

More importantly, they discovered that unlike newspapers, radio was the first effective means of communication that reached the opposition's supporters. So great an effect did this simple observation have, that newspapers themselves began to lose their partisan leanings in order to compete, and the long, slow process of separating the voter from traditional party loyalties began.

Radio in the 1920s became part of the US information apparatus, although in Britain Sir John Reith (Managing Director) stoutly resisted Churchill's efforts to commandeer the BBC during the General Strike. Coolidge caused a sensation when he delivered the first broadcast State of the Union address. Excited groups of citizens crowded around office and shop radios as the President spoke live from the Capitol. In 1928 the Republican and Democratic parties' conventions were being broadcast on the radio and it had become an election campaign tool. But it was still comedy shows like *Amos 'n' Andy* (sponsored by Pepsodent) that America stopped work to listen to; that is until Roosevelt's fireside chats. It was during his time as New York State Governor that Roosevelt became such an excellent radio performer, allowing him to exploit the medium's true potential to help him into the White House. Roosevelt's professionalism was uncanny. Working for several days on a speech (because, he told impatient aides, it was the most important work he could possibly do), he would memorize it, reading the words aloud to himself. Then, after the NBC man tapped his shoulder to signal they were on, with that relaxed but strong, full voice, he would begin, 'My friends ...'.

What he said was personal, both in terms of content and style. He spoke slowly as if to a friend on the telephone (something most modern politicians have still failed to master), informally and warmly, calming their fears of economic hardship. When the Republicans criticized him, he evinced no anger but reported simply that his dog Fala's 'Irish was up' at his opponents' attitude. He spoke of his family and his home life. If it was hot in the Oval office he would ask his audience to excuse him for a moment and turn to an aide to ask for a cooling glass of water. Hearing him in their own homes (or in a neighbour's if they did not own a radio), the effect was electrifying on the people. The president was speaking to *them,* them *personally.* Citizens wrote to 'their friend' in droves, 4000 letters a day (one hundred times the amount Hoover received). The networks clamoured for more, but Steve Early, presidential press secretary, turned down the offer of a weekly broadcast saying that people can't stand the repetition of the highest note on the scale for long.

Radio reporters became more and more powerful. One day when the *New York Times* and *Chicago Tribune* reporters got into the second car following the president's (wire services were in the first) they found the CBS and NBC correspondents already occupying it. Their protests to Early did no good: CBS communicated to more citizens and voters than the *Times* and *realpolitik* demoted the press down the presidential motorcade. They never got their place back.

## Moving pictures

When Roosevelt had finished his chat, the Oval office doors would open and in would troop the newsreel cameramen with their noisy equipment. For the cinema was just as powerful a medium for his New Deal policies as radio and, in a wider context, even more important. Indeed, Lenin said 'Of all the arts, the cinema is the most important for us'.

The first British moving pictures were recorded in January 1889 by William Friese-Greene in Hyde Park (at the spot where, 48 years later, the first BBC outside broadcast took place at George VI's Coronation procession). From that moment until television was widely available in the 1950s, it was cinematography that was the image maker's most ubiquitous weapon. When Queen Victoria was persuaded to pause on the steps of St Paul's on the day of her diamond jubilee and pose for pictures by the new 'cinematograph' machine, they were not as great a success as the Jubilee itself was. But Victoria thought they were 'very wonderful' if a 'little hazy and too rapid'. During the Boer War a novel news format was developed, films that showed the events of the period. The first ones were faked on Hampstead Heath with actors playing the South African guerillas, but by 1908, Pathé in France were running regular 'news reels' as these little films were called.

By 1910 5-cent theatres were frequented by 26 million Americans every week. Only three years later Hollywood made its first feature film, *The Squaw Man*, directed by Cecil B de Mille. The enormous power of stars like Chaplin, Fairbanks and Pickford was subsequently harnessed by the US government to sell war bonds, and after the sinking of the Lusitania in May 1915, with many US citizens aboard, Hollywood was happy to co-operate in movies like *The Little American* that reinforced stories of German atrocities. The cinema grew up in the same year with its first masterpiece, David Wark Griffith's *Birth of a Nation* (the first film to be shown in the White House and adjudged by President Wilson to be 'like writing history with lightning'). This introduced image makers to film 'grammar', eg 'cross cutting' (showing alternate shots of different scenes); 'switcheroos' (suddenly cutting to another scene and revealing new facts to heighten suspense); 'yaks' (a funny surprise); and 'bleeders' (a pathetic surprise). The image makers (but not the audiences) learnt that the camera lies like a trooper, especially by juxtaposition and omission. Today's image makers owe enormous debts to the Hollywood studios, who developed three key techniques: the makeover, hype and scandal management.

## The makeover process

The studio managers took waitresses and truck drivers and made them 'stars'. This process of 'makeover' was not just a question of improving physical attributes like teeth; hair; physique; make-up and so on, but also coaching in voice (after the coming of sound in 1927); accent; correct reading material; deportment; singing; riding and fencing; the 'right' car, pets and boyfriends. 'Svengalis' did a brisk trade in the creation of superstars. Mauritz Stiller manufactured Garbo out of a Stockholm shopgirl; Josef von Sternberg invented Marlene Dietrich, and Natacha Rambova fashioned pure sex out of Rudolph Valentino.

Press agents reinvented family histories, ran fan clubs, produced fan magazines that sold millions of copies and ghosted the stars' 'autobiographies'. They also came up with the stars' best lines, like Monroe's famous answer to a reporter's query (about her soft porn calendar posing) as to whether she had anything on at the time. Her press agent told her to reply 'Yes, the radio'. And, disappointingly, most of Goldwyn's malapropisms (eg 'We can get all the Indians we want at the reservoir') were actually invented by Pete Smith, his press agent.

By the 1930s, these stars were more influential than politicians and their every move was scrutinized. When, in the film *It Happened One Night*, Clark Gable took off his shirt and revealed he did not wear a vest, every red-blooded male in America went home and quietly got rid of theirs – causing havoc in the garment industry. Both the hat trade and the tobacco barons promptly hired lobbyists to ensure movies never featured stars hatless or appeared on screen without a cigar, a pipe or a cigarette permanently glued to their lips.

## The art of hype

Although Hollywood did not invent 'hype' (P T Barnum probably deserves the credit), the studio publicity departments made it into an art form. The greatest of all the publicity czars was Russell Birdwell, who became famous for carrying out a completely bogus nationwide search for an 'unknown' to play Scarlett O'Hara in *Gone With the Wind*, in the process hyping the movie to saturation awareness before the public had even seen a frame of film.

## Keeping scandal under control

Men like Birdwell were also experts in a specialist form of news management – the suppression of scandal. From the moment that the stars' names were featured on screen (Florence Lawrence 'The Biograph Girl' was the first in 1910) their private lives gave the studio chiefs ulcers. While Clara Bow 'entertained' the entire USC football team (known as the 'Thundering Herd'),

Wallace Reid injected himself with morphine (supplied by the studio to make sure he completed shooting on time) and comedian Roscoe 'Fatty' Arbuckle was arrested and tried for rape and murder after a wild party in a San Francisco hotel room. Some stars were not quite what they appeared on screen.

At one time Cary Grant was living with Randolph Scott while having an affair with Howard Hughes on the side. His publicity adviser managed to keep both relationships out of the papers. Homosexuality, drug and alcohol addiction, promiscuity and adultery all had to be kept out of the media to protect the studios' investment in the stars. Their exposure had to wait until 1975 and the publication of Kenneth Anger's books on Hollywood.

## All-American values

Given their vulnerability to scandal, Hollywood's own image makers were keen to cooperate with the government and other important institutions to reinforce 'American values'. The Roman Catholic Church looked fondly on such movies as *Boys Town* and *Going My Way*. Bio-pics of Lincoln and Disraeli flattered politicians. In Frank Capra's *oeuvre*, for example (which is one long advertisement for the American way of life), Jimmy Stewart triumphed over evil tycoons in *It's a Wonderful Life* and corrupt machine politicos in *Mr Smith Goes to Washington*.

However, it was in the depiction of law enforcement that Hollywood's efforts shone brightest. It all started with Alphonse 'Scarface Al' Capone. Out of the Chicago gangster wars of the 1920s, Capone emerged as a media celebrity; part myth, part psychopath and all-American businessman. In an outrageous pastiche of the stereotypical tycoon, carrying a cane and yellow deerskin gloves, wearing spats, a rose buttonhole and an 11½-carat diamond on his ring finger, Capone used to leave his home at the Hawthorne Hotel with 18 tuxedoed bodyguards (more than the president), enter his armour-plated limousine and drive to his office on South Michigan Avenue, preceded by a motorcycle escort and followed by another car full of armed guards – to the excitement and awed fascination of the Chicago citizenry. Through a combination of bribery of politicians, police, lawyers and reporters; intimidation; and modern business methods, Capone had amassed a huge fortune (his income in 1928 was £105 million) and attracted Hollywood's attention through the enormous publicity he sought and received. After *Little Caesar* in 1930, Hollywood mined a rich vein of gangster-dom, glamorizing them by using Jimmy Cagney and George Raft – while carefully providing the obligatory sticky end to satisfy the Hays Office censor. Fifty gangster movies were made in 1931 alone.

## The 'G-man' cycle

The antidote to this celluloid crime wave did not take long to arrive, in the form of John Edgar Hoover who, in 1924, at the age of 29, had become director of the Federal Bureau of Investigation. Hoover, anxious to increase his funding and establish the FBI, was a very sophisticated image maker on its (and his own) behalf. Although crime actually dropped between the two World Wars, Hoover took advantage of the wild hysteria Hollywood was inducing (along with famous real-life incidents such as the Lindbergh baby kidnapping) to build up those villains he would then destroy.

FBI agents got their name by a piece of Bureau press department embroidery following the arrest of 'Machine Gun' Kelly, who, the press people claimed, shouted in a panic, 'Don't shoot, G-Men, don't shoot.' (What he actually said was, 'OK boys, I've been waiting for you all night.') This incident taught Hoover two valuable lessons in news management. The first was that the press will turn whoever it thinks is in charge of a case into a hero – so Hoover let it be understood throughout the Bureau that he was to be described as being in personal command of every important case. The second was that reporters tended to base their stories on the interpretation given out by the first high-ranking official who managed to get a statement to the press, so Hoover always made sure that he was ready with unembargoed press releases whenever a big story broke.

Hoover then formed an alliance with a freelance reporter called Courtney Ryley Cooper, who was the creator of the FBI image we still know today. Hoover opened his files to Cooper, who wrote 3 books (one of them ghost-written for Hoover), 24 short stories and 4 movie scripts. All featuring real-life Bureau cases and portraying the FBI as an incorruptible, courageous, scientific and professional force that would improve the standards of policing and provide facilities that were beyond local police forces, such as fingerprint files, crime labs and statistical services.

In 1935, Hollywood took this formula and developed the 'G-man cycle' of movies, notably *G-Men* itself, with Cagney playing the lead. Radio serials and comic strips followed, all sponsored by the Bureau. Hollywood had made Hoover so famous and powerful that he could now elbow the attorney-general and the Justice Department aside and stand alone as the only direct expression of the US public's anger against the gangsters. He was to remain as director of the FBI until his death in 1972 at the age of 77. And to this day, Hollywood still makes films and television series about the Bureau, for example *Feds*, a 1980s film about women agents. This symbiotic relationship is still a strong and mutually profitable one.

### Goebbels – the first real image maker?

Twelve thousand kilometres away in Germany a movie buff called Paul Josef Goebbels studied Hollywood's methods with excitement and fascination. In fact, Goebbels even made strenuous efforts to persuade his idol, Marlene Dietrich, to return from Hollywood to work for the Third Reich. To her credit Dietrich refused.

Although, of course, it is not now mentioned in polite society (and especially not in the Institute of Public Relations) Goebbels' claims to be the first, fully-fledged image maker are impeccable. Although he cut an unimpressive physical figure, Goebbels turned himself into a brilliant public speaker and a successful writer of propaganda.

In 1926, Hitler appointed him Berlin's National Socialist Gauleiter, just before Goebbels' 29th birthday. Like both his master and Mussolini, Goebbels was heavily influenced by the theories of psychology, especially crowd psychology. He read Le Bon's book *About the Psychology of the Masses* so often he knew long passages by heart. Both he and Hitler were also inspired by both the early Communists' communications skills and the British First World war propaganda machine. Hitler had studied advertising techniques and concluded that consistency and perseverance were the twin secrets of success. Impressed with the sea of red flags, red armbands and red flowers that the Berlin Marxists used in their parades, Hitler sought a design that would symbolize National Socialism. Taking as his starting point the 1871 black, white and red Imperial flag, he chose a red background which he said 'expressed the social thought under-lying the movement'; on which he placed a white circle, symbolizing 'the national thought'; and superimposed a symbol borrowed from the German Workers Party – the Hakenkreuz or swastika, signifying the 'struggle for the victory of Aryan mankind'. It also had the benefit of being easy to reproduce easily by crude printing methods and ubiquitous graffiti in the dust of windows and vehicles (an advantage it had over Mussolini's more complex fascio).

Hitler believed that the spoken word was more effective than the written and, together with Goebbels, he set about using the technology available to him to excite the masses into enthusiasm for his drastic solutions to Germany's economic problems. Albert Speer, at his trial, observed that Hitler's was 'the first dictatorship in the present period of modern technical develop-ment, a dictatorship which made complete use of all technical means for the domination of its own country. Through technical devices like the radio and the loud speaker, 80 million were deprived of independent thought.'

With the invention of the microphone and public address loudspeakers, it was then possible for Goebbels to stage-manage mass meetings with audiences in the hundreds of thousands. After warm-up speeches, Hitler would arrive to the strains of Wagner overlaid with the sound of hundreds of drums. Applause manipulation facilities were built into the design of the Nuremberg stadium by wiring strategically positioned micro-phones to amplifiers hidden behind the rostrum (and from the Riefenstahl's cameras). Technicians would then beam back the crowd's own applause and shouts of '*Sieg Heil*', until the real and artificial formed a colossal spiral of sound. Germans at home could sense the excitement through radio broadcasts. The speeches were also recorded on tiny gramophone records which were inserted into envelopes and mailed to supporters. Another Goebbels first, not used again until 1959 for Macmillan's speeches.

Goebbels had trained and rehearsed Hitler in the early days, coaching him out of a naturally poor speaking voice and emphasizing dynamism as a style to which Hitler should aspire. Hitler's oratorical model was David Lloyd George, although he never achieved the latter's subtlety of language. As Hitler needed glasses to read, Goebbels had special large type scripts prepared for all public occasions. The coloured lighting and gigantic stage sets were borrowed from Expressionism and the theatrical atmosphere was enhanced by the profusion of uniforms.

The content of the speeches was based on the propaganda principles outlined so lucidly in *Mein Kampf.* The words must, Hitler said, 'appeal to the feelings of the public, rather than to their reasoning powers'. Both he and Goebbels exhibited (privately) utter contempt for the German people, believing that simple slogans aimed at the lowest intellect, persistently repeated, would be successful. It is an extremely uncomfortable thought for those who believe in democracy, that these methods were so successful. Hitler likened the process of the individual sublimating that individuality to the crowd, as similar to the psychological shelter and comfort a soldier derives from his platoon, where he feels 'the strength of his comrades'. Lies were their stock in trade. Hitler had outlined the theory of the 'big lie' (so big no one could credit anyone being capable of fabricating such a colossal untruth) and Goebbels 'sophisticated' the idea by the simple injunction 'when you have told a lie, you must stick to it'. This was said when, after the sinking of the Athenia (two days after the outbreak of war, with the loss of 128 lives) by a German U-boat, Goebbels claimed that in fact it had been carried out on the orders of Churchill in order to drag the US into the war.

These lies and smears, particularly the gross calumnies of the Jews, were communicated in the 1932 elections through all the technological developments now familiar to us: posters, films, newsreels, newspaper articles, leaflets, radio and so on. Having gained power in 1933, the Nazis' focus switched away from the domestic population (who could, if they would not be persuaded by Goebbels' Ministry of Propaganda and National Enlightenment, be beaten or gassed into submission) to persuading the people of Britain and America of the Nazi cause. Goebbels installed short-wave radio stations to broadcast German language programmes worldwide, bought shares in American newspapers to control their editors, and wrote articles for the *Sunday Express*.

Goebbels' direct influence on image makers who work within the democratic process today is slight, but his theories and technical innovations are still used by those who wish to tyrannize their people into blind obedience to a totalitarian state.

## Television – That miracle of electronics

When in 1939, at the New York World's Fair, Roosevelt addressed a small audience, the speech went by almost unnoticed, yet it signalled one of the most important changes in 20th-century politics. For the first time in history, American citizens could see their president as he spoke, while not being present; if, that is, they were one of the few who owned that miracle of electronics – a television set.

### *A political career saver*

The first politician that television made into a national figure was Senator Estes Kefauver, due to the broadcasting of his fascinating committee hearings on organized crime in 1951. This pretend hick (he affected a coonskin hat *à la* Davy Crockett) was in fact a Yale law school graduate from Tennessee, who was the first to understand that television would turn the primary system for presidential elections into the key to winning the nomination at the convention. So impressed were party bosses with his television performance that they gave him the vice-presidential spot on the Stevenson ticket, edging out the young Massachusetts senator, John Fitzgerald Kennedy.

Television was also responsible for saving the career of Richard Nixon. On 18 September 1952, a headline on the front page of the *New York Post* read 'Secret Rich Men's Trust Fund Keeps Nixon in Style Far Beyond His Salary' and called for his resignation. Eisenhower was caught between confirming Nixon's place on the election ticket and saying nothing, so he left it to his vice-president. Nixon and his media adviser, Ted Rogers (former Hollywood and CBS producer), advised that a half-hour at prime time following the Milton Berle Show be bought and he set about building a 'library' set (an idea much copied since) and devised what he called a 'preventive TV' angle system which consisted of a large, shallow oval, outlined in white on the studio floor. Rogers coached Nixon to stay within the oval and thus within shot. As the programme opened Nixon was fighting for his political life, a drowning man going down for the third time. Thirty minutes later he was a Republican hero and firm candidate for the vice-presidential position ('Ike Keeps Vindicated Nixon on the Ticket' read one headline the next day.)

Nearly 50 per cent of the available television audience saw Nixon 'bare his soul'. In an intensely personal talk, he described his early married life in modest circumstances, and his current house payments, and the dog he received as a gift that his children named Checkers, saying 'You know the kids love the dog' and (with dark glances at his Democratic critics) 'we're gonna keep it'. Far from wearing a mink coat, as some reporters had alleged, he claimed his wife Pat wore 'a respectable Republican cloth coat'. Most importantly, he alleged that Adlai Stevenson, the Democratic candidate, had a secret fund of his own. At the end of the broadcast Nixon, emotionally over-wrought, buried his head in the 'library' curtains and cried, saying to Rogers, 'I'm sorry Ted. I loused it up.' He could not have been more wrong. The effect of this coast-to-coast appeal was stunning. Two million telegrams, letters and phone calls were received at the Republican party HQ, running 350 to 1 in Nixon's favour. Eisenhower had no choice: Nixon was quickly confirmed as his running mate.

From the start politicians scrambled both to buy time on the new medium and to hire what were called 'television advisers'. It wasn't long before Madison Avenue itself entered the political fray. One day three rich Republicans were playing a round of golf and chatting about the depressing fact that the Democrats' slogan 'You never had it so good' (later appropriated by Harold Macmillan) seemed to be very effective. They decided that their own party needed its own snappy slogan and called the legendary Rosser Reeves of the Ted Bates Agency.

Reeves was famous for the invention of the unique selling proposition (USP), which sought to communicate the differential advantage that every brand must have to succeed. His book, *Reality in Advertising*, was a bestseller in the business world and he built the agency up to be the world's Number 2 by making a leader out of brands like Colgate Dental Cream, 'It cleans your breath, while it cleans your teeth'. (So does every other toothpaste, of course.)

## 'Eisenhower Answers America'

Supervised by Eisenhower's advertising agency Batten, Barton, Durston & Osborne (once unkindly described as sounding like a man falling downstairs), Reeves argued that now sufficient numbers of Americans had TV sets (18 million homes, 39 per cent of the total) that a 20-second 'spot' advertising campaign 'Eisenhower Answers America' be run. The format was simple: a member of the public stood looking off camera and asked Eisenhower a question about taxes, Korea, communism, food prices and so on, as advised by George Gallup, the pollster. Cut to Ike, who answered briefly but crisply, while being careful not to commit himself. These answers were written by Reeves on to giant, hand-lettered cue cards which Eisenhower read (without his glasses).

Between takes, Eisenhower shook his head sadly and complained, 'To think that an old soldier should come to this', but in all, 40 of these spots were filmed at the Transfilm studios in Manhattan for a cost of $60,000 and aired up to four or five times a day in 40 states for an air-time cost of less than $1.5 million.

## TV in Britain

In Britain, the television service had started in 1936 to tiny audiences – Ramsay MacDonald had installed a set in No 10 Downing Street to watch John Logie Baird's closed circuit experiments, but the output was mostly trivial light entertainment, ignored by the political establishment and public alike. A glimpse into the future was obtained in 1938, when the BBC's outside broadcast cameras were present when Chamberlain returned from Munich and inaugurated that entertaining series of unhappy-with-hindsight one-liners, 'Peace for our time'; 'the pound in your pocket' (Wilson); 'cutting inflation at a stroke' (Heath); 'crisis, what crisis?' (Callaghan); 'rejoice, rejoice' (Thatcher); and 'if it's not hurting, it's not working' (Major).

After the war ended and the television service resumed, the parties went out of their way to attempt to circumscribe its influence. The 14-Day Rule was enforced, which meant that no subject that was uncertain, or even likely to be debated in the House of Commons in the following fortnight, could be discussed on television. Party election broadcasts similar to those on radio were rejected out of hand and, under self-imposed restrictions, the BBC did not even report the existence of the 1950 General Election campaign.

Eden made the first and very successful election broadcast in 1951 (a faked interview, learned by rote, with the popular television personality of the time, Leslie Mitchell), but Churchill treated television with aristocratic disdain, and Attlee promised to strangle ITV at birth if Labour won power in the 1955 election. Radio still ruled the roost until well into the 1950s when John Profumo, Central Office's first head of broadcasting returned from the 1952 US presidential election. He had been struck by television's enormous political impact and he convinced Churchill that television was 'the real thing'. Although Eden was surrounded by television experts hired by Central Office, it was not until the arrival of the actor-manager Macmillan that television's potential for persuasion was fully explored.

## Supermac

Macmillan himself was subjected to the now standard Hollywood 'makeover'. Out went the baggy trousers and in came well-cut suits from Savile Row. Out went his Red Commissar spectacles and his snaggled and decaying teeth. The Colonel Blimp moustache was ruthlessly pruned and the hair restyled in a more distinguished and sophisticated cut. After a course of television training at Conservative Central Office, which was not entirely successful, the former BBC controller, Norman Collins, was hired to produce Macmillan's media appearances and the comedian Bud Flanagan was brought in to coach him in acting.

Soon the cartoonists (starting with Vicky) were ironically calling him 'Supermac', not realizing they were contributing to an image of an all-powerful prime minister incapable of error, at ease with and on top of the job.

He allowed himself to be interviewed by television reporters at Heathrow, coming and going from his many foreign trips, although no face-to-face interviews in the 1959 election with him or Gaitskell were permitted. Macmillan's television coup was to persuade outgoing President Eisenhower to appear with him in a live television discussion just before the start of the British General Election campaign. The president and the prime minister sat in the state drawing room in an orgy of mutual admiration, before ambling off to an adjoining room where the camera recorded their dinner guests (which included Sir Winston Churchill) breaking into enthusiastic applause.

The image of a national leader above party politics and on first-name terms with the most powerful, popular and respected leader in the West was extremely effective. Macmillan had understood one simple and vitally important fact about the new medium: *how* you look is as (sometimes more) important as *what* you say. On the other side of the Atlantic, his dinner guest's deputy was about to learn the same lesson but in a particularly harsh fashion. As David Brinkley said, 'When you get in front of the camera, you get out of the news business and you're into show business.'

### *Kennedy v Nixon*

*In the modern presidency, concern for image must rank with concern for substance.*

Richard Milhous Nixon

The moment the primacy of the image over the word in the control of political power was first recognized and acknowledged by politicians, can be traced back to a single day, 26 September, 1960, in an old converted sports arena, the CBS studios at McClurg Court, Chicago. On that evening, a young, inexperienced senator debated with a two-term vice-president of the USA, and won. The way John Kennedy was prepared for the debate by his image makers was in stark contrast to Nixon's preparation, and now makes a textbook case study for any image maker.

[31]

Kennedy's preparation was characterized by what Theodore White called 'his typical attention to organization and his air of casual self-possession'. His personal brains trust spent all day flinging questions at him in a relaxed but purposeful way, as the candidate lay on his bed in the Ambassador East Hotel dressed in a white T-shirt and chinos, and were questioned in turn. His staff had prepared fact cards to meet any probable eventuality and, as each issue was dealt with, Kennedy would send them spinning off to the opposite wall.

Refreshed from his usual afternoon nap, he ate dinner, dressed in a white shirt and dark grey suit, asked for a stop-watch and drove to the studios to meet his 29-year-old media adviser, Bill Wilson, who had spent all day chatting to his old colleagues at WBBM, the CBS affiliate, and ensuring the lighting, set and other conditions were right for Kennedy. Bolstered by the Californian sun and a touch of Man Tan, at first Kennedy refused to wear any studio make-up, fearing that reporters waiting outside the make-up room would note it and compare it to Nixon's lack of camouflage. Wilson was firm: the senator needed some kind of make-up, mostly to close the pores and keep the shine down. Kennedy paused, look at his adviser and asked him, 'Do you know what you're doing?' and, satisfied with Wilson's confident 'Yes', told him to arrange it. Wilson left the studio, ran two blocks to a pharmacy, bought a Max Factor Creme Puff and proceeded to apply a light coating to Kennedy's face. When he sat for the camera on the set for his adviser's inspection, one of the CBS producers interrupted and told Kennedy that his white shirt would produce glare under the intense lighting. The Senator sent an aide back to the hotel room to fetch a blue shirt, which he then put on.

Over in the Nixon camp, his media adviser, Ted Rogers, had done his best to make conditions favourable to his boss. Worried about the deep eye shadows cast on Nixon's face, he requested two tiny spotlights called 'inkies' be shone directly into the eye wells. (In the event, even this went wrong. A group of stills photographers were allowed on the set and they knocked the lights out of position.) He successfully demanded that no shots be taken of the vice-president's left profile or of him mopping sweat from his face. Rogers had, however, a particularly severe handicap to overcome: he had not talked to or even seen the candidate for months.

Nixon had accepted the debate because he was afraid a refusal would become a campaign issue, but he was unprepared physically or mentally for the ordeal. He was worn out and suffering from a two-week stay in hospital following a nasty knock to his knee. Ten pounds underweight, his collar was now a size too large and it hung loosely around his neck (a fact Rogers was unaware of).

Despite frantic calls which failed to pierce the Berlin Wall of H R Haldeman (Nixon's chief aide), Rogers's efforts to get to Nixon failed. Not only did Nixon arrive late on Sunday (after a bruising and psychologically depressing encounter with the United Brotherhood of Carpenters and Joiners), but he stayed in his hotel room at the Pick-Congress all day, alone and incommunicado. Finally, Rogers persuaded Nixon's entourage that he should be allowed to travel in the candidate's car for the ten-minute drive to the studios. In the car he urged Nixon to come out swinging to see if he could knock Kennedy off balance with the first punch, but Nixon refused.

Rogers was shocked by Nixon's appearance, but knew it was too late to do anything about it. As they left the car, Nixon struck the same injured knee on the car door and paled. Inside the studios, Nixon, like Kennedy before him, refused any make-up, but Rogers persuaded him to cover up his five o'clock shadow with Lazy Shave; while the pores on forehead and upper lip were left untouched, with disastrous consequences.

Seventy million Americans watched as Kennedy stood erect, calm, crisply outlined by his dark suit against the grey 'scale 5' background, speaking energetically to the audience in their living rooms, rather than to his opponent or the questioning reporters. By contrast, Nixon slouched to relieve the pain in his knee, his Lazy Shave streaked with sweat (a process encouraged by Wilson who had found the studio thermostat in the basement and surreptitiously turned the dial up); black hollow eyes and dark stubble on his jowls. He glanced furtively to the right, where the studio clock was, while Kennedy, when not speaking, always looked intently at Nixon (checking the effect from time to time on the studio monitor).

Kennedy seemed to throw off the charge of immaturity with ease – after all, there he was standing toe-to-toe with an incumbent vice-president and trading punch for punch. Nixon's image of the shifty, second-hand automobile dealer was simply reinforced. In the control booth there was pandemonium. The CBS team were terrified that Nixon's appearance would be held against them. Wilson kept insisting they show more and more cutaways to Nixon, while Rogers yelled at the director to have more close ups of Kennedy – anything to get away from that awful picture of Nixon on the gallery monitors.

At the end, *The Post* and the *St Louis Dispatch* called it a draw and those (like the southern governors), listening on radio gave it to Nixon, but the post-debate polls among those who watched it on TV were clear: Kennedy had won.

Kennedy's crowds immediately multiplied, the people turning out to see this new TV star. While Mayor Daley's stuffed ballot boxes probably were the vital factor in his victory, the pollsters calculated that two million votes switched to Kennedy during the debates and, given he won by only 112,000, it's not surprising he said later, 'It was TV more than anything else that turned the tide'. Certainly Pierre Salinger (Kennedy's press secretary) thought that his election would have been 'impossible without the effect of victory in the first debate'. The statistics were as follows. Fifty-seven per cent claimed the debates had influenced their vote, 6 per cent said the debates *alone* decided their vote. In all, 120 million people watched one or more of the four debates (more than had watched any event in history), beating the previous record of 90 million who watched the final games of the 1959 baseball World Series.

Nixon, in his memoirs, pointed out that the nature of television – with its emphasis on physical appearance over substance – was what hurt him most. He observed that, since the advent of television as the primary means of communication and people's source of information, modern politicians must have special talents, at once 'more superficial and more complicated' than those of their predecessors – in order to manipulate the media, while avoiding at all costs the charge of *trying* to manipulate the media.

The one-eyed image makers were now kings in the land, their technical expertise transmogrified in the minds of politicians to a magic wand. In fact, the debate was won by a combination of rehearsal, preparation and attention to detail – the rules that still apply today.

## *The TV royals*

By the 1960s, most politicians had grasped both the raw power of the medium and its cruel nature, its 'hot, pitiless, probing eye', as Macmillan put it. They had also learned that this power gave television the confidence to intrude into every area of power, even (after Profumo) into the private lives of the powerful – and few resisted. Except that is one group. Not the most powerful perhaps, but to many the most interesting and easily the most private – the royal family.

There had been 'court newsmen' since George III's day, but it was only in 1947, after the Second World War had ended, that a press secretary became firmly established at the Palace. The first of these was Commander Colville, whose idea of image making is summarized by his pithy view that 'My job is for the most part to keep stories about the Queen out of the press'.

One of the first times BBC outside broadcast cameras had been used was for George VI's coronation, but an unholy alliance of Churchill and the Earl Marshal (the Duke of Norfolk) nearly won the battle against Reith's view that the experiment should be repeated in 1953. Queen Elizabeth herself eventually settled the row by sending Churchill away with a royal flea in his ear. A cowed and resigned cabinet at once agreed to her desire for the coronation 'to be seen by people everywhere', but ordered that the cameras be kept at least 30 ft away from the Queen. The BBC promptly substituted 12-in lenses (rather than the usual 2-in) and shot the Queen in close up – without telling the Earl Marshal.

Television had proved itself a perfect medium for royal pageantry and Christmas broadcasts (the first was in 1958). But the private life of the royal family was still hidden from their subjects' gaze, that is until 8 pm on 21 June 1969, when the image of the House of Windsor was changed suddenly and irrevocably. That night the BBC was showing *Royal Family*, a 105-minute documentary made by a consortium of BBC and ITV person-nel, produced and directed by Richard Cawston. The deal had been struck by the Queen's new Australian press secretary, William Heseltine, in response to endless requests to film the royal family 'at home' and 'let daylight in upon magic', to use Bagehot's phrase. The Palace denied that it had been made as a public relations exercise, but of course that's exactly what it was – and a highly successful one at that.

The film showed for the first time a prime ministerial audience; the acceptance of the US ambassador's credentials; Prince Philip painting, and flying a helicopter; Prince Charles with President Nixon (*Nixon* [jovially] 'I've seen you on television.' *Prince Charles* [coolly] 'I've seen you too.'), a family picnic at Balmoral (*HM Queen* [hinting] 'Well, the salad is finished.' *Duke of Edinburgh* [sarcastically, while grilling sausages] 'Well done. This, as you will observe, is not.'); as well as a visit to the village sweet shop by the Queen and Prince Edward in search of an ice cream.

From the moment the press applauded spontaneously at the preview showing, the programme was a stunning hit. The BBC's research showed a sharp increase in those describing the Queen as 'outspoken, powerful, approachable and lively'. *The Times* compared it with George V's historic innovation, the first Christmas broadcast. The mystique and the remoteness was destroyed for ever. In its place, the commentators said, came 'natural dignity' and a 'human and relaxed approach'. The papers were also quick to point out that despite Heseltine's denials that it was the film's objective, it showed very clearly the advantages of the monarchical system (with special reference to the version operated by the House of Windsor) to a press which still felt the need to compare the merits of a constitutional monarchy with those of an elected head of state.

The real appeal of the film was revealed in the choice of *The Times'* headline 'Queen Prepares Salad while Anne Grills Steak'. The nation watched in fascination as, for the first time, the royal family entered their living rooms as 'real people', individuals with the same kinds of quirks, personalities and habits as the rest of us.

This approach was repeated, again successfully, in the BBC *Elizabeth R* documentary shown in February 1992. The nation watched agog to see Her Majesty actually running delightedly to collect her £16 Derby sweepstake winnings and peering out at the flocks of tourists outside her palace windows.

Television had proved it was so powerful that it could command the Sovereign herself. Indeed, the wedding of the Prince of Wales to Lady Diana Spencer took place in St Paul's Cathedral for the simple reason that it facilitated better camera angles than Westminster Abbey. Television had decided that it had a right to intrude into the private lives of the powerful (the grief-stricken would be next on the list) and that its responsibilities were to report everything that editors decided was 'news'. Now it was these people, rather than the powerful, who would decide. At this point enter the image makers, the powerful's answer to television's heady mixture of power and threat.

2

# First impressions

*It is only shallow people who do not judge by appearance.*

Oscar Wilde

Modern image making is divided into three disciplines: the personal; marketing; and news management. In this chapter I deal with the first of these, ie how physical appearance, background and personality combine to produce an image. Communication in politics and business mostly consists of taking ideas and expressing them through words and pictures. As people are often the means of transmission of these ideas, it is impossible for their personal characteristics not to be important. As viewers and readers we cannot help but react to another human being in a pre-programmed way. We react on a psychological level, both by using instincts buried deep inside us from our tribal past and by comparing the subject we view with various cultural norms. Our intellects may sometimes suspend their disbelief, but our atavistic instincts are triggered involuntarily. Through repeated exposure to a person, we build up a library of information on them – including, of course, our own remembered reactions to them. It is the image maker's job to make sure that that library contains only suitably positive reading material. This they can do by changing the physical appearance of the principal (person, brand, organization) and choosing which aspects of their background or personality to publicize.

In the same way that any job seeker puts their best foot forward at an interview, or any house vendor cleans their home before showing the prospective purchaser around, image makers select those aspects of the person that chime best with an audience's ideas, attitudes and beliefs. Barristers coaching their 'innocent until proven guilty' clients don't usually instruct them to volunteer information prejudicial to their defence. Are these job seekers, house vendors and barristers all lying? By omission, certainly. Should we throw the first stone? I doubt it. Certainly image makers who lie about or on behalf of their clients are fools, and naïve fools at that. Lies are unnecessary (one can always say nothing) and are invariably found out.

The good image maker simply tries to identify the positive aspects of the principal and emphasizes those.

## First impressions last ...

Let's get one thing straight from the start about physical appearance. Arguing that it *shouldn't* matter is a perfectly sensible and valid position to adopt. But, arguing that it *doesn't* matter is plainly silly. Some recruitment managers, for example, often maintain that they never take physical aspects into consideration, only experience and ability. In my experience this is pure baloney.

Many politicians and businesspeople know perfectly well that appearance counts, but they normally resent that fact and often stubbornly refuse to seek or take advice. They would rather spend their time thinking up ingenious arguments why personal appearance is either unimportant or irrelevant. Even the experience of watching this attitude backfire on others is sometimes not enough to sway them.

Common sense, empirical observation and science all tell us that appearance does indeed matter. The saying 'first impressions last' is (as are most clichés) largely true. By observation everyone knows for example that, when better dressed, they receive superior service in shops, restaurants and when travelling.

As Peter Gummer (chairman of Shandwick and one of Britain's most experienced image makers) says, 'The way somebody looks is more important than what they say – no question about it.' And Michael Jones (political editor of *The Sunday Times* and an experienced observer of politicians) points out that, especially since the advent of television, '*how* it's said is as important as *what* is said.'

It is perhaps depressing when science reveals more exactly our dependence on appearance. In Professor Mehrabian's study, *Silent Messages*, we read that the impact we make on others depends on the following: how we look and behave – 55 per cent; how we speak – 38 per cent and what we say only 7 per cent. Content and form must therefore synchronize for, if they don't, form will usually dominate or undermine content.

The speed at which we make our judgements is also increasing as our exposure to television teaches us to understand the meaning of complex visual signals in 10 and 20-second news or advertisement 'bites'. Today's children interpret those signals at even greater speeds than this. This shortening of our attention span is often taken by the chattering classes to be symptomatic of a lack of due thought, but, as Harvey Thomas (an image maker to Billy Graham and Margaret Thatcher among many others) wisely observes, the message to those in the public eye should be 'You have to earn the viewer's attention, it's not a right.'

## 'Placing' people on the social map

Because of increased social and job mobility we now meet more and more strangers, learning to 'place them' on our private map of the world by noting their physical attributes – such as voice, accent, face, hair, teeth, make-up, height, weight, disabilities, state of health, energy levels, posture, body language, and by the 'props' they have – such as clothes, cars, jewellery, and the food and drink they consume.

As we get to know them a little better, their personal background is revealed: their education; religion; political principles; class; income; occupation; clubs; societies; parents; spouse; children; relatives; friends; close advisers; colleagues; hobbies; pets; preferred sports and so on.

Lastly, on greater exposure and intimacy, something of their personality emerges: humour; temperament; experience;

truthfulness; moral integrity; self-discipline; self-esteem; ethics; intellect; charisma; leadership skills; taste etc.

Nowhere is this facility for the judgement of strangers more significant than in the world of power, because the powerful (unlike the soap opera star or the sports personality) control our lives. They do this by making promises to us which, if they are to be believed, will either change our lives for the better, or retain the good things that already exist. We are forced back on our perception skills in order to make a judgement about the credibility of these promises, because we know from experience that the intellect is not effective on its own.

## Lessons from Hollywood

The first lesson that the image maker learns about appearance derives, as so many others do, from Hollywood. The studios learnt that it takes a tremendous amount of artifice to appear 'natural'. When objects like the human form are represented to the eye through any other medium than air, they are distorted and it is the image maker's job to bend them back into shape. So, for example, in advertising, liquid chocolate is often brown paint; baked beans and ice cubes are usually made out of plastic; and food is painted with glycerine to replace the moisture sheen that lights dry out. Steam is hard for the lens to pick up, so hot meat pies are often treated with cigarette smoke. Colours do not appear as they do in real life, so vegetables have to be boiled in acid. Blonde, brown, purple and some reds close to the 'rare earth' red in the TV tube are avoided because they are all difficult to reproduce – the human eye being infinitely more subtle and effective than film emulsion or electronics.

Make-up has to be used to counter the effects of lighting and close-up lenses. Shadows and skin folds are painted out and pores filled in to smooth the skin. The effects of human physiology have to be taken into account. One sometimes sees in studios hand and leg models draining the blood from their veins by holding their hands up above their shoulders or by lying with their legs above their heads. Some photographers make their models stay up all night rather than try to mask the puffiness we all have in our faces after sleep.

The electronics of television also cause problems because they cannot scan images as effectively as the eye. Clothes with checks or horizontal stripes often appear to move as the scanner dithers between which line to place them on, producing moiré inter-ference patterns. Despite all these years of television you still see businesspeople and politicians wearing totally unsuitable clothes (eg houndstooth check jackets, or shirts with narrow stripes) to interviews.

TV cameras can only see contrast in a ratio of 4:1, so white shirts often produce 'burn out' as the camera tries to deal simultaneously with the white and a dark suit.

## Improving on nature

When we meet someone for the first time we normally look at their face first (as it is uncovered), then body, and then, finally, clothes. We listen to their voice as they say 'How d'you do', and feel the warmth and sweat of their hand, while gauging their strength by its pressure on ours. At the same time we analyze – largely unconsciously – their body language and the 'props' they carry about with them: jewellery, handbags, cigarettes, wallet etc. The image makers realize the importance of these impres-sions and are constantly trying to ensure that physical attributes are not distracting from or undermining the message. And when they do, action sometimes has to be taken.

### *The eyes have it*

Most people *believe* that they can 'read' personality from faces. Indeed, Khrushchev once memorably described Nixon's face as one of 'A petty shopkeeper, capable of selling tainted herring'. But the most important part of the face they use to read people is the eyes. Proust said, rightly, that 'the eyes are the organ through which intelligence shows'. They are also the most reliable indicator of the personality since they are almost never artificially altered (with the exception of coloured contact lenses). In the US there is now a small band of highly specialized 'jury consultants' who are used to weed out jurors who may be hostile to the defendant. They claim to rely heavily on the eyes to

[43]

divine prejudice. Eyes are also especially important when one individual is trying to discover whether another likes them, as our pupils dilate when we look at someone to whom we are attracted. Many professional recruiters swear by their ability to pick the right person from a study of their eyes.

Although failing eyesight is common as we grow older, the powerful are often reluctant to wear glasses in public, for fear of hiding their eyes. Kennedy, Nixon and Reagan for example, wore glasses, but never on television.

## Under the knife

Pretty much everything else can be changed by image makers with scalpels in their hands – the cosmetic surgeons. Up to 15 years of ageing can be removed by surgery. An 'upper third' lift gets rid of crow's feet and brow furrows, while liposuction eliminates neck wattles, bags under the eyes and paunches. Silicone implants are used to strengthen the jaw, cheeks and buttocks, and to increase the size of calves, breasts and pectorals. Collagen is used to make the lips more full.

Rhinoplasty is now a common operation (especially among men) to reduce the size of the nose. Surgery is used to reduce the effects of age and to beautify, and is increasingly being used as a substitute for psychotherapy. A facelift cannot stop the ageing process, but it can take years off a person's face, making them look healthier, which is why those professions that depend on looks have always used surgery (along with diet and exercise) as an aid to keeping their jobs. I've always thought that a light tan is the best cosmetic for the face, however. When Coco Chanel started the fashion for *bronzage*, she gave the world a cheap (and, if not taken to excess, for it is burning of the skin and not tanning, that causes malignant melanoma, relatively safe) way to look healthy.

Surgery can also be used to improve the look of the teeth. For example, Roosevelt needed a special false tooth to eliminate the whistle that was produced by the gap in his upper front pair and which the radio microphone picked up. Cosmetic dentistry was started in the late 1920s by a man called Charlie Pincus, who set up shop in Hollywood to service the needs of the studios. His successor as the leading cosmetic dentist is an Englishman, Philip

Kurland, who runs a Harley Street practice. Pop stars, actors, politicians and businesspeople all come to Kurland's surgery in order to increase self-confidence and to get the youthful, healthy (and friendly) look they want. Teeth can be capped, cleaned and polished to preserve a healthy whiteness.

As it is the teeth that do most to maintain our facial structure, at least of the lower part of the face, loss of our teeth, or badly fitted dentures and bridges, produces that characteristic 'Punch' look of the elderly.

Cosmetic dentists can even change the way a patient's personality is perceived. For example, bringing the two upper canine teeth forward produced a more masculine, even aggressive, look in men. Since the early 1960s many senior politicians (including all prime ministers) have been the subject of cosmetic dentistry. Increasingly, businesspeople are following this example, prompted, no doubt, by the immaculately capped teeth of their US and German colleagues.

## *The importance of hairstyle*

After wigs had gone out of fashion in the 1790s, hairstyles became more natural, yet they still communicate aspects of class and personality. For example, one newspaper editor once told me he hated a particular minister. I asked him why this was. He said he'd never met the man, but knew from his hairstyle that he was an 'upper-class twit'.

An untidy haircut like that of Michael Foot is often interpreted as showing a lack of self-discipline. An overly ornate one like General Custer's may betoken vanity.

Some styles scream at the viewer that the person is fighting hard against time – and losing. Kennedy experienced the opposite problem. He had to have his hair trimmed during the 1960 election campaign to reduce its 'college boy' style, making it less bushy to add years. Reagan was habitually (and wrongly) accused of dyeing his hair to reverse the ageing process, finally succumbing to the desperate strategy of offering the sweepings of his barber shop floor to be analyzed.

When toupees are worn, they signal the triumph of vanity over realism and objectivity – did you ever see a wig that looked like anything other than a wig? Small wonder then that, in the

US, these hairpieces are the subject of 'outing' campaigns. We could do with a similar campaign here to get rid of those ludicrous 'comb the last few remaining strands from over the ear' styles. Whoever told Neil Kinnock to own up to baldness was doing him a great service.

## Fitness and health

Clearly the health or otherwise of the people we meet or see on television plays an important part in our assessment of them. For, as Zola wrote, referring to Napoleon III's bladder stones, 'a grain of sand in a man's flesh and empires falter and fall'.

Obesity is a particular problem nowadays, because what used to be seen as a sign of success and well-being is now taken to show self-indulgence and weakness of character. My definition of a 'fat' man is one whose waist exceeds his chest.

Image makers have a long history of covering up bad health for fear that it might be interpreted as unfitness for office. After Woodrow Wilson's stroke in 1919, the US was effectively run by his wife and his doctor. Roosevelt's paralysis from an attack of polio when he was 39 (and not syphilis, as was rumoured during the 1932 election) was assiduously covered up by his image makers. Steve Early, his press secretary, ordered the White House press corps never to take photographs of the president in his wheelchair or on crutches and, for the most part, they complied. When the cameras were present and standing was unavoidable, callipers were used and he would stand supported by his son's arm. Inside the White House he would simply be picked up by a secret service bodyguard and carried.

In the 1930s Baldwin's constant nervous disorders were concealed from the voters, as was the syphilis that both Hitler and Mussolini suffered from (the Fuhrer in addition suffered from Parkinson's disease). Photographers were ordered to shoot Stalin from the right, so hiding his shortened left arm. It was Mussolini's aides who started the fashion for faking Stakhanovite work rates by pretending Il Duce worked on the nation's problems far into the night. In fact, they simply left the lights on in his office overlooking the Piazza Venezia long after he had left for the day.

Gorbachev's diabetes was well concealed from the Soviet citizens, as was John Kennedy's Addison's disease. When Winston Churchill suffered a stroke while presiding over a state banquet in No 10, observers assumed he was drunk and he was spirited away to Chartwell, out of reach of photographers who might recognize his doctor, Lord Moran. A false impression was then given of the gravity and nature of his illness. By 1954, one year later, Churchill, it was reported, could no longer follow discussions in cabinet.

Sometimes this kind of concealment is not possible, especially if a serving head of government needs to visit hospital. Eden's biliary fever and Macmillan's enlarged prostrate could not be hidden for this reason, and both prime ministers resigned because of their health problems.

Most political and business leaders are as strong as oxen and serious breakdowns are comparatively rare. In modern times, the late Lord Armstrong, head of the Home Civil Service, suffered a complete nervous breakdown, accompanied by religious mania. After he recovered he took the post of chairman of Midland Bank. So successful had the cover-up been that not even the other directors knew of his illness.

In Gerald Ford's case the reverse of the norm was true. A gifted athlete, he slipped descending from Air Force One while guiding his wife down the runway steps. This was immediately seized upon by a delighted press and satirists like Johnny Carson and Chevy Chase. Remarks about playing too much football without a helmet followed, and gradually the public's perception of Ford became one of a clumsy, slow-witted man.

While Margaret Thatcher (by my observation) existed solely on a diet of black coffee and walking everywhere very fast, Reagan kept himself fit by exercising with weights every afternoon at 5 pm. Fit though Reagan was, few people realized how profoundly deaf he was until they saw his hearing aid (which had to be specially 'swept' for KGB bugs at regular intervals). Contrary to rumour (and unlike the youthful Kennedy), he did not nap in the afternoon. His main problem was that, when he delivered speeches perfectly, his performance was dismissed as simply that of a professional actor, yet when he fumbled it was taken as a sign of incipient senility.

[47]

The 'Ageing Rights' movement helped blunt the criticism of the media, who were becoming wary of crossing the 'politically correct' line on ageism. For example, when Reagan turned 69 on 6 February 1988, between the Iowa caucus and the New Hampshire primary, his image makers publicized his birthday party, defying Carter and Bush to make an issue of his age. Both opponents backed off and little more was heard on the subject.

Reagan's early ads in the 1980 election were deliberately shot on film in order to light his face to make him look younger. Having made the same mistake when filming Margaret Thatcher once in 1989, I would recommend that great care is taken when using make-up, lenses and filters to reduce ageing. I had arranged for one of Britain's top photographers, Terry Donovan, to film her on 35mm for a party political broadcast. He (along with Barbara Daly, the number one make-up artist) made Mrs Thatcher look wonderful, but when I showed the finished film to voters in focus groups they all said that she looked 'unreal' and that maybe what she was saying was false too. I realized that the 'reality' for the voter was the image they saw which was produced by the harsher lighting used for video cameras in news studios and that we had to achieve an image congruent with that version.

Near the start of his premiership John Major was the subject of rumours about his health. Overwork, it was said, was the culprit. Conservative Central Office added fuel to the flames by refusing to release an official portrait, because he looked too tired on the day it was taken. Unwisely, his wife gave an interview to a local newspaper which did nothing to quell these rumours, which were promptly given even more substance by George Bush's comment that the prime minister looked 'wiped out'. Bush himself, despite being very fit for his age, has been the subject of repeated health scares. Getting enough sleep is always a problem for political and business leaders and it is no coincidence that a great many of them belong to the 2 per cent of the population who need only five hours or less.

## The super-liars

What sends out the greatest signal of health is enthusiasm for the job, but we also give out signals that, try as we might, sabotage our displays of enthusiasm. The image makers' interest in 'body language', as these signals came to be called, started with the publication in 1967 of *The Naked Ape* by Dr Desmond Morris, and his subsequent book, *Manwatching*.

Morris posited the thesis that all our gestures and postures transmit messages. This bodily activity, he claimed, is a throwback to our 'animal' past and cannot be hidden. Even more alarming than this, he said that we are all equipped to interpret these movements; that is, to discover their hidden meaning. Until the coming of television the powerful had little to fear from a close observation of their body language – other than obvious 'autonomic' signals such as yawning (boredom), sweating (fear) or blushing (embarrassment or sometimes rage). The advent of television gave the experienced and aware observer a chance to match the words of the speaker with the constant and revealing accompaniment of hand, eye and body movements.

Morris explains in *Manwatching* the concept of 'nonverbal leakage', ie involuntary actions which betray our true feelings. For example, hand movements, he says, are particularly telling, especially the use of a hand covering the mouth or touching the nose, which reveals the fact that a verbal deception is probably being practised (ie someone's lying). Morris points out that the legs and feet are an even better give-away, which is why we sometimes feel uncomfortable without the use of a 'screen' like a desk or table.

Reassuringly (for the image makers), Morris also points out that those he called 'super-liars' (like diplomats, politicians, barristers, conjurers, conmen and used-car salesmen) could learn to become adept at what is called contextual manipulation, ie choosing the right moment to lie. The image makers made the obvious conclusion from this: that what can be learnt can also be taught. The result is a mini-industry of preparing people in the public eye (from Prince Charles, cabinet ministers and captains of industry to public relations officers and company flak-catchers) by teaching them how to mask their body language.

A great deal of interview training is devoted to stopping the principal from revealing his or her nervousness, by eliminating these revealing movements, rather than offering training in actual deception. A knowledge of certain 'masking' techniques

[49]

is, however, useful to the tyro public speaker or interviewee. Below I have given two simple examples.

### 'Gaze behaviour'

'Gaze behaviour' involves the non-verbal clues we give out and receive when looking at another person. Sexual interest, hostility and anxiety are all revealed by the length of time we spend with our eyes locked. We glance constantly at the person we are talking to and away from them, to check their reactions. And as we are the only primate to develop a large area of white around the pupil, this serves to make these glances very conspicuous. In normal conversation the eyes only meet when one speaker is handing over to the other. We can all discern, for example, a shifty individual by the unnaturally nervous fluctuation of their eyes. Interviewees are therefore trained to look sincere by steadily looking at the interviewer's eyes. This is made possible by staring directly at the bridge of the nose, which the interviewer cannot distinguish from eye-lock.

Similarly, to hold the audience's attention public speakers are taught to treat the audience as individuals, sweeping the audience slowly and achieving eye-lock with each person for a very short time, but at regular intervals.

Newscasters are taught to avoid staring constantly at the rolling autocue (which produces the 'super-stare' of hostility), and to glance down at the script notes occasionally to relieve the tension which constant eye-lock with the viewer causes.

### 'Status displays'

The other example is an altogether more subtle manipulation of body language, which *is* intended to deceive. 'Status displays', Morris explains, are devices used to reinforce status and induce submission, which have superseded physical power as a method of establishing a pecking order in business. He cites the wearing of immaculately polished, hand-made shoes; the absence of office paraphernalia like briefcases; the refusal to operate machinery such as telephones; full diaries, full waiting rooms and the surrounding cocoon of private secretaries, bodyguards, chauffeurs and other body servants.

[50]

Here again, the image makers instantly grasped that what is understood can be copied. Soon grooming consultants joined the growing band of advisers that surrounded the powerful, to ensure that the correct status display signals were being given out. They also earned themselves fortunes by advising those lower down the pecking order how to simulate these displays and therefore appear to have the qualities of the powerful. To do this they advise on the right 'props' that these business 'actors' need.

## Powerful props

The powerful have always used 'props' like clothes (the senatorial toga or the bishop's mitre); jewellery (the papal ring); furniture (the imperial throne); weapons, animals, buildings, vehicles (Air Force One), to reinforce their power. Further down the scale their equivalents are the country seat, the tycoon's yacht, the company jet, the chauffeured limousine and the opulent office (such as Mussolini's famous Sala del Mappamondo which was 60 intimidating feet from door to desk).

Clothes have been used for every conceivable image objective throughout history. Alexander, having conquered the Persians, relieved their humiliation at having to submit to his imperial designs by adopting Persian dress. When Queen Victoria visited Ireland shortly after the famine and risked the jeers of the mob, Lord Clarendon turned the visit into a PR triumph by insisting the Queen wore dresses of good Irish linen, on which she displayed a large sprig of shamrock. The Irish were suitably charmed by this regal condescension.

As the three great tyrants, Hitler, Mussolini and Stalin, were 5 ft 9 in, 5 ft 6 in and 5 ft 4 in respectively, they all wore specially designed uniforms to improve their somewhat insignificant civilian appearance. Mussolini went one step further and copied Napoleon (5 ft 4 in) by parading superciliously on horseback.

Real soldiers are not above glamorizing themselves by similar methods. George Patton emphasized his reputation for speed and panache by toting twin ivory handled revolvers, while his more cautious rival, Bernard Law Montgomery, emphasized his

originality and informality by wearing civilian clothes dotted
with an eccentric collection of regimental insignia.

Politicians have long used clothes to attract votes, US politicians being particularly partial to wearing a succession of Indian
headdresses, yarmulkes, stetsons and steel hats to emphasize
their solidarity with various groups of voters. Lloyd George
underlined his Celtic roots by carrying a shepherd's crook and
wearing a dramatic, flowing black cloak. Churchill's air of
insouciant sophistication derived partly from his ever-present
Romeo y Julieta, while his reefer jacket gave the home front
civilians a reassuring reminder of his naval expertise. Harold
Wilson's thoughtful pipe contradicted the notion that here was a
dangerous radical, but rather a steady, Baldwinesque kind of
cove, calmly grasping the tiller of government. Nowadays
politicians still smoke, but they tend to hide their pipes (Kinnock) or cigarettes (Ashdown) when the cameras appear.

In business, Sir John Harvey Jones borrowed the Bohemian
look of long hair and shocking ties to emphasize both his
individuality and his dislike of ICI's pompous hierarchy, while
Richard Branson wears woolly jumpers to give himself the air of
a man close to his student entrepreneur roots.

## Dressing to impress

One of the best clues to judging personality (after face and body)
comes from a person's clothes. They convey detailed and subtle
messages about us which our audience has become extremely
skilled at interpreting.

For the masses, the importance of style in clothes started after
the First World War, when society leaders began to express the
*zeitgeist* in part through the way they dressed. Magazines showed
the ordinary citizen that fashion need not be prerogative of the
moneyed classes. Men were given permission to be more stylish
by the example of the then Prince of Wales. He dispensed with
the traditional frock coats and spats (at one of the 1926 garden
parties at Buckingham Palace, piles of spats were found in the
shrubbery, discarded by embarrassed guests). He also dispensed
– much to the King's irritation – with old-fashioned side creases
in trousers and introduced both the Windsor knot and the zip to

polite society. He wore suede shoes (even worse, with a blue suit) and not just in the country.

Men (and their wives) went to the movies and saw those kings of style Fred Astaire and Cary Grant and tried to copy them. Astaire, for example, had a horror of clothes looking too new, which he thought unstylish. To his valet's annoyance his solution was to throw them repeatedly at brick walls until they became suitably 'weathered'.

In politics Anthony Eden was the role model for the right, debonair in the Lock's homburg that bore his name and his elegant Stowel and Mason 'Eden Silhouette' suits. Keir Hardie, for the left, entered the Commons in a tweed cap and black lounge suit (instead of silk hat and frock coat). Both before and since, the left have been fond of expressing their leanings through unorthodox clothing, eg the *sans culotte* revolutionaries in France in 1789 and Mao jackets in China in 1967.

On the stage, Noel Coward lounged in Sulka's best dressing gowns, and in the office, lounge suits (which were descended directly from hacking jackets) became universal – literally so, as they replaced national dress for the progressive middle classes of many emergent Third World nations.

Post-war austerity and a conformist spirit then took over and the 'Our Age' generation dressed solely to signal membership of their societal group (and thought it important to do so), providing a very different model to the Clapham omnibus passenger than the stylish Thirties generation had done.

Eccentrics and Bohemians were tolerated up to a point but, as soon as anyone suggested that one might dress to please, impress or persuade those not in their peer group, scorn and derision were the order of the day: scorn for 'trivializing' political life, and derision because this practice was seen as narcissistic, with probably effeminate undertones. Hair was cut at Truefit and Hill, suits made in Savile Row, shirts in Jermyn Street, and ties were club, regiment, school or college. The bottoms of trousers were worn rolled. Detachable collars, waistcoats and hats were *de rigeur* (along with an air of effortless social and intellectual superiority, mostly undeserved).

The 'My Age' generation started (as with so many other things) with Kennedy. He wore button-down Brooks Brothers Oxford shirts and wing-tip brogues, with suits cut by the

legendary John King Wilson. Most importantly, he did not wear
a hat, thus making a stark contrast with the ageing Eisenhower.
Even Macmillan in England, was quick to copy this particular
expression of youthful modernity (they also shared the same
tailor) and no senior western politician – other than Enoch
Powell – has been seen to wear one since.

Reagan played the same hatless trick on Gorbachev at their
first meeting in Geneva. Reagan (the older man by 20 years)
bounded down the steps of the conference venue to shake the
Russian's hand wearing only a suit. Gorbachev looked awkward
and old-fashioned in his overcoat and scarf.

The clothes sense of both sexes was liberated even further in
the 1960s (especially in the sense of individuality and casual-
ness), but it was in the 1980s that the pre-war interest in style was
reinstated. Magazines like *The Face* were launched, along with
chain-stores like Next. Style gurus educated us in 'power'
dressing and what 'Sloane Rangers' wore. In the spirit of that
time certain clothes became associated with success (shoulder
pads) or nerdish failure (white socks). The wearing of casual
clothes increased even further, especially of 'alibi' clothes, that is,
sports clothes worn by people who did not use them for sports,
eg trainers and tracksuits. The younger working class abandoned formal clothes altogether, except for special occasions.

Among the politicians, George Bush now wears casual clothes
at Kennebunkport news conferences. John Major is obviously
more comfortable in informal clothes and manages to carry off
this approach well. For example, some thought had obviously
gone into the wardrobe he wore in the Gulf (a cable-knit, sand-
coloured sweater and chinos). He has, however, avoided the
charge of lack of gravitas which Michael Foot's appearance in a
'donkey' jacket at the Cenotaph ceremony brought about. The
outrage following this incident taught politicians a lot about
'sense of occasion' and the definition of informality – which does
not include untidiness or indifference.

### Choices express personality

The media constantly reinforces in the mind of the 'person in
the Clapham company car' (to use Michael White's phrase) a key
lesson of the age, ie clothes convey messages because they

involve (to those with the money to pay for them) choices, and those choices express personality.

Because image makers understand that clothes convey an extraordinary amount of information about the wearer, they are able to select which bits of information about their principal they wish to communicate, by making specific choices for them. Class, status, taste, style, fashion sense, occupation, nationality, rank, can all be communicated through a particular style of clothes. More importantly, personality – especially on the innovative to conservative spectrum, can be communicated by what the powerful choose to wear.

When John Major became prime minister many articles appeared in newspapers concerning his clothes and appearance because journalists were seeking clues to his personality. The front page of the *Sunday Times* following his election featured an article written by the political correspondent which suggested how he could be 'made over'. This brought a swift reaction from Downing Street. 'I shall be the same plug-ugly that I always was', was followed by, 'People will have to take me as I am', and 'The image makers will not find me under their tutelage'. All of this was considered by No 10 to be a useful way of amplifying his 'honest John' image.

However, by the following spring, double-breasted Chester Barrie suits had replaced the shapeless originals, new (non-reflective) spectacles were being worn and his hair tidied up. But it was too late – the media had decided he was 'grey', 'a suburban banker', 'bland', 'faceless', 'nondescript' or 'boring'. The British Shops and Stores Association claimed he was setting an 'appalling example' and dressing 'like an old man'; his clothes, they said, 'were a complete bore'.

Major was in the grip of a phenomenon that affects many senior male executives when they suddenly reach the top. For years they jog along with only their wives or mistresses caring very much what they look like, until promotion throws them bodily into the media spotlight. They are rarely trained to handle this experience and are often shocked to find that, having appeared on television, most of the comments they receive on their performance pertain to their appearance and not content. Because of all this, it is important for politicians and businesspeople to appear both in touch and modern in their approach, and clothes play a vital part in this – to the dismay of those who would rather politics and business lived in a more intellectual milieu.

## Tieing up the personality

For men the tie is probably the most potent expression of personality – indeed, just wearing a tie at all now signifies much. It also gives men a chance to bluff. Neil Kinnock, for example, has taken to wearing 'regimental-style' ties which convey an image of manliness and integrity. Ties offer a way of conforming to the tribe's mores (club, school, society or university) or of expressing a desire to be different (floral, hand-painted, vivid patterns etc). It is said that Freud even considered wearing a Paisley tie to be connected to self-images of virility (owing to the pattern's supposed resemblance to sperm), which sounds both apocryphal and ridiculous. Both material and knots are much discussed – madder silk and an Olney knot are best, the experts claim, especially for keeping the tie in place when TV clip-on microphones are being used.

So important is the tie in corporate America that the *Wall Street Journal* regularly briefs its readers as to what the current 'power' tie colour and pattern is. In a few days, Lower Manhattan is a sea of ties of the prescribed type. The only time Kenneth Baker and I ever fell out was over his Woosterish penchant for wearing floral or otherwise unsuitably vivid ties in important television interviews. He claimed that they expressed his individuality. I maintained that not only were they ghastly, but they also distracted the viewers' attention.

## Shiny shoes show style

Shoes, in my view, are also a wonderful window on to the personality, not the style or quality of them (which is mainly to do with money), but their condition. The first thing I ever noticed about Neil Kinnock, when we used to pass each other in television studios, was the brilliant gleam from his highly polished shoes (and I'll wager the soles were polished too). This gave one a clue to the fact that he is, in fact, more self-disciplined and organized than might usually be thought.

# Good Grooming

Image makers in Britain came late to 'grooming', possibly out of a very British reserve about giving advice on personal matters. Gordon Reece advised Mrs Thatcher not to wear hats on television, but her clothes were left to such informal advisers as her daughter, Carol, and Cynthia Crawford, who were none the less extremely effective in producing a consistently smart and fashionable appearance.

A leading consultant on grooming is Mary Spillane, a Harvard Kennedy School graduate who worked as a policy adviser in Carter's White House. Her consultancy advises clients on their personal appearance using simple principles of colour and psychology. A great deal of Spillane's grooming advice consists of the elimination of negative impressions. In Britain, this mainly takes the form of instilling a sense of 'appropriateness' (which is the guiding light of a class-ridden society such as ours), rather than style or status. This means getting rid of men's sartorial solecisms such as grey shoes, white socks, polyester ties, matching handkerchiefs, clip-on braces, cufflinks in single-button cuffs (a Kinnockism) and tinted spectacles. For women it means removing white shoes, fake tans, plastic earrings and peroxide hair with 'roots'.

Spillane says she is in 'the self-esteem and the confidence business' because better grooming gives an impression of health and youthful energy, which leads to increased self-confidence – a similar rationale to that used by cosmetic surgeons.

Spillane's *modus operandi* comes in two parts. The first is akin to the observational methods of an artist: material, cut and colour. The client is told whether they fall into one of four tonal types: 'Winter' (pale skin, dark hair, brown eyes); 'Spring' (ivory skin, blonde hair, blue eyes); 'Summer' (ivory skin, red hair, brown eyes); and 'Autumn' (pink skin, blonde hair, blue eyes). They are then advised on the colours that match these tones. For example, Neil Kinnock is an obvious 'Spring' type, so he would be better off not wearing his over-large, double-breasted, dark suits and white shirts, which would tend to bleach the colour out of his face, and make him look tired and older than his actual years.

The psychological properties of colour cannot be proved, but psychologists have shown in tests that some colours do seem to

[57]

radiate authority (blue and grey), approachability (brown, Reagan's preferred choice) and so on. Such experts are now employed by companies whose products depend on correct colour choices; for example, Tom Porter researches ties for Tie Rack, and Desmond Morris develops paints for Dulux.

The second mode of operation of Spillane is based on a mixture of sociological and psychological theory, and practical tips on hair styles, make-up, accessories, shopping and so on. Spectacle wearers will be advised on the right colour, thickness, material and bridge type to wear (this last is used to correct too widely or too closely set eyes, and to lengthen or shorten the nose).

In a society that provides ever greater opportunities for everyone to rise in it, there will always be a growing body of men and women who did not receive this kind of social instruction at home or school, as the moneyed classes did. How to behave in a restaurant is a typical example – which wine to order, which fork to use etc. Now all this may seem trivial to many who take their own (mostly unconscious) training for granted, but if it puts people at their ease, I'm all for it. Perhaps it is mild fakery, but it seems a harmless patina of the 'come up through the ranks to the officers' mess' variety.

Compared with this, the manner in which lawyers transform their dubious defendants into facsimiles of respectable and law-abiding citizens should be regarded as nothing less than fraudulent conversion. As long as these image consultancies don't simply encourage homogeneity and do emphasize individuality, I think they can provide a minor but useful weapon in the armoury of image making.

## The voice – An underrated asset

If bodily appearance and clothes are important factors in increasing your credibility, the voice is even more significant. In my view, voice is a tremendously underrated asset of those in power, who very often make the mistake of ignoring its effect. Properly trained, it can be a most reliable and effective weapon in conveying an image of confidence, credibility and authority. Moreover, it can be taught quite easily and, unlike so much

[58]

image making, the changes that have been made are hard to detect by anyone other than professional voice experts. Philippa Davies is a leading voice coach, who teaches people in the public eye how to breathe properly, how to regulate pitch and improve articulation. Most voice problems are caused by breathing problems, as voice is simply breath striking the vocal chords. The most common problem image makers have to contend with in their principals is breathing too quickly, especially when answering questions in an interview. Their need for approval and fear of the viewer's interpretation of any hesitation makes them rush in when a slight pause is needed. Training to rectify this problem is fairly simple and involves the 'I pause and I breathe' method to slow the word rate down, giving a related and more authoritative tone. Other problems may be postural. For example, Neil Kinnock constantly thrusts his chin forward when speaking for 'flight or fight' reasons. This causes serious throat and vocal chord tension and can lead to an unnatural emphasis on words. In these cases Alexander technique treatment may be necessary.

Another useful technique is 'deep' breathing. By breathing from the bottom of our lungs we take in eight times more oxygen than from the top and therefore we can speak for longer. This prevents interruptions from the interviewer, which are triggered by the very slight breaks in speech flow that occur when we pause to take in more oxygen.

## Pitch and resonance

Voice coaches are also very useful in improving pitch and resonance, as these colour words with meaning and authority. Lyndon Johnson, for instance, imported voice coaches from Hollywood to improve his resonance, with great effect. Some orators (Lloyd George, Mussolini, Reagan) have naturally sonorous voices, but the rest of us have to learn it from others, like any other skill. Pitch patterns (that is the musical 'note' of our voice) are listened to with great care by an audience. For example, a rising inflexion is often understood as meaning doubt. Pitch drops pose a particular problem as they suggest tentativeness on the part of the speaker. Learning to use rising pitch is useful as it is an excellent way of turning propositions into suggestions.

Probably because we still associate masculinity with authority, a deeper-toned voice, Davies says, is considered more confident and authoritative, so for men with comparatively high pitch, and most women, the pitch can be lowered by exercises designed to raise the pharynx at the back of the mouth. This 'excessive pharyngeal resonance' was used by Mrs Thatcher when she received voice coaching recommended by Gordon Reece. This reduced the electronic reading of her voice to 46 Hz, which is the level approximately half-way between the average male voice and the female average.

Resonance (the use of available air space in the body) also affects tone. John Major is a typical case of 'nasal resonance' speech, which is both phonetically unpleasant and generally inexpressive (I know, I suffer from it too). This is very often caused by physiological problems such as sinus trouble. We express vowels through the mouth and consonants through the nose. If too much air passes through the nose then vowel sounds become lost and the result is the very thin resonance typical of south London speech.

You can test yourself quite simply by pinching the nose between forefinger and thumb. Now say 'man'. The 'a' should sound distinctly; if it doesn't then it means you are habitually passing too much air out through the nose.

### Effective articulation

Speech therapy can be useful to increase articulation – speech being defined as what happens in the mouth cavity and lips. Davies reports that the most common problem for the British is the 'stiff upper lip' syndrome. To articulate properly the muscles in the upper lip need to be flexible – which is the reason Prince Charles sounds so strangulated.

In interviews the facial muscles tend to freeze owing to nerves, and the strain of keeping the muscles in the same place causes them to twitch. Muscle relaxation exercises are often provided for businesspeople who have to appear on television to use just before the interview takes place. This is very useful because trust in the interviewee is increased as the facial features become more expressive. In addition, facial expressions can be used to keep the interviewer listening and, therefore, not interrupting.

Intensity of articulation is provided by coaching in voice projection, although this does not increase the volume of sound as is sometimes mistakenly thought. Instead, as with actors' soliloquies, greater intensity increases the feeling that the speaker is confiding in the audience. It is an especially effective technique on radio, where intimacy is at a premium. Both President Reagan and Mrs Thatcher had a particular talent for this type of voice projection and were both better on radio than on television.

'Confiding' is also particularly relevant when appearing on television from a 'remote' studio with the interviewer miles away at the broadcasting station HQ. It is a disconcerting experience for most people, because although one can hear the interviewer's voice, often they cannot be seen. One tends to declaim, even shout, as we do when talking on a telephone, and the stridency of the voice sounds unpleasant and is often interpreted as hostility or annoyance. The solution is to confide in the audience by imagining that a familiar person is the recipient of your answers – your spouse or a colleague, for example. If possible, the principal should not look directly into the lens, but across it to an aide, and speak to them. This is also useful in preventing the principal nodding when in fact he disagrees with the interviewer's point. A shake of the head from the aide during the question will provide a reminder to the principal not to begin their answer with 'Yes, but ...' when they really mean 'No!'.

### Accents on power

Before radio, accents were, of course, rarely commented upon, but in 1928 (the first year the Republican party earmarked the majority of their advertising budget for radio) Governor Al Smith was upbraided in the press for pronouncing 'first' in his native, East Side way as 'foist'. Hoover was also criticized, but for his affectation in using the English pronunciation of 'speciality'.

Coaching in accents is much rarer than it used to be, as we now accept a greater range of accents in public life than before. Regional accents among the powerful in Britain were comparatively rare until recently, as most were educated to speak 'received pronunciation' standard English. Peel spoke with a broad provincial accent. He was ashamed of it and tried to cover it up, but without success. As George Bernard Shaw said 'It is impossible for an Englishman to open his mouth without making some other Englishman despise him'.

The days when would-be television presenters with broad regional accents would lock themselves in their university rooms, emerging later with a cut-glass version, are mostly gone. John Major may say 'wunt' for 'want', but he generally speaks in the accents (and vocabulary) of the civil servants that have surrounded him since the beginnings of his career.

The most interesting use of accent nowadays is 'mockney', a false version of east London speech used in a reverse of the Eliza Doolittle process to create an image of 'man of the people'. Especially popular among pop stars, it is used well by Mick Jagger, but badly by Nigel Kennedy, the violinist, who was brought up in a perfectly ordinary middle-class home.

Demotic usage in politics can be traced back to the extraordinary success among the book-reading classes of the Thames Television series *Minder*. We now hear the chairman of the Conservative and Unionist party demanding that the Labour party stop telling 'porkies' (pork pie = lie) and the Hon William Arthur Waldegrave (Fellow of All Souls) saying in his 1991 Blackpool Conference speech, 'nice one Arfur'. All of this is about as convincing as Mr Patten preaching Thatcherite principles or Mr Waldegrave visiting a Happy Eater.

## Background and all it entails

Background, especially in a country like Britain, which has a long history of division by class, is just as important an aid as physical attributes are in coming to a judgement about others. By background I mean birthplace (or at least where one was brought up), parents, class, education, religion, siblings, spouse, relatives, friends, income and occupation. In terms of the governing élite, class is still by far the most important criterion.

### Birthplace

The first of these, birthplace, has often been taken to be an indelible sign of political leanings. For example, in the US the

Harrison–Van Buren presidential contest in 1840 produced the first personal image advertising based on background. The *Baltimore Republican* of the day disparaged Harrison's fitness for office, saying he would be perfectly content with just a 'log cabin and a jar of hard cider'. Harrison's image makers quickly converted this sneer to his advantage, using it to identify their candidate (who was the wealthy son of a state governor) with the rural working man. Alarmed by the success of this 'log cabin' strategy, the Democrats responded by publicizing the fact that Harrison actually owned a lush 2,000-acre estate in Indiana upon which stood his palatial mansion. Unimpressed voters went on wearing their log cabin badges and handkerchiefs, while waving their log cabin banners – and voted the incumbent Van Buren out of office.

Now some have subsequently said that this could never happen today as the Bernstein/Woodward inspired media would expose the fraud. I wonder. Remember Carter in his work shirt and denims inspecting peanuts on his Georgia farm, or Reagan splitting wood on his California ranch, or even Margaret Thatcher washing dishes in Flood Street? None of these images were faked, but none were exactly a documentary reflection of the lives that leaders actually led – nor could any such photo-opportunities possibly be.

## A taste of class

We decipher class signals easily and they signify a great deal to us – especially those to do with 'taste'. When Harold Macmillan first 'emerged' as leader of the Conservative party, the newspapers were full of the fact that he had celebrated with his chief whip (Edward Heath) at the Turf Club on a meal of champagne and oysters. Journalists saw this as evidence of Macmillan's rather Edwardian penchant for ducal living and contrasted this to (the loser) Butler's plain and frugal style.

Similarly, when Harold Wilson took over, much was made of his insistence that HP sauce should be present on the dining table, this being taken as evidence of the 'common touch'. Wilson was a master at this kind of image making. He smoked a reassuring pipe in public and large cigars in private. He drank beer in working men's clubs on the campaign trail, but brandy (a capitalist running-dog drink if ever there was one) at home. He holidayed on the Scilly Isles (playing golf), as any ordinary, respectable petit bourgeois clerk might, whereas he was in fact a left-wing Oxford don with a First in PPE, who was president of the Board of Trade at 31.

The enduring quality of food to create an image was proved yet again after John Major was elected Conservative party leader and he stopped (on the way to the Young Conservatives' conference) at a Happy Eater restaurant outside Doncaster. This, coming on top of his expressed desire for a 'classless society' (whatever that means), was taken as irrefutable evidence that he retained the habits and instincts of his humble background.

Labour weren't quick enough in thinking up an answer to 'classlessness' (eg does it mean the abolition of the aristocracy and the honours system?) and the No 10 image makers quickly 'sophisticated' the word to mean 'open and meritocratic'. In fact, his father was a small businessman in the suburbs, the name he insisted he was called by until adulthood was John Major-Ball, he went to grammar school and subsequently became a banker. The difficulties of a prime minister trying to convey a 'classless' image are illustrated by a subsequent opinion poll in which 89 per cent expressed the view that Major was in fact 'middle class'. The equivalent score for Kinnock was 78 per cent (while Mick Jagger's was 52 per cent). His habit of eating fry-ups on camera was not new, however. When he was an almost unknown junior minister, he allowed himself to be filmed having breakfast in the Italian cafe on Marsham Street, presumably with similar intent. George Bush has not had the same success in creating a suitable image in a country that at least imagines itself classless. When Bush was 'accused' of being born in the 'rich folks county' of Connecticut, he claimed that he couldn't help it, he 'just wanted to be near his mother'. He is a 'preppie' and always will be, but he has nevertheless developed a good line in self-deprecatory references to his extraordinary circumlocutions, once facing down his critics with the jokey challenge, 'Go ahead, make my twenty-four hour period'. To redress the balance he has, however, used his Texas connections to evince a love of Tex-Mex food, the chilli-dog being the near equivalent of egg and chips in working class Hispanic America.

Certainly the most ruthless use of class to destroy an opponent came in the Conservative party leadership election in 1990, when the most experienced, intelligent and personally impressive candidate, Douglas Hurd, was utterly destroyed by charges made by the Major camp that he was unsuitable owing to his social background. Faced with the dread accusation that he was in fact a toff, Hurd pointed out that he was the son of a tenant farmer and could not have studied at Eton without the help of a scholarship. It was all to no avail, Hurd later lamenting bitterly, 'I thought I was running to be leader of the Conservative party, not some demented Marxist outfit.'

## Education (or lack of it)

John Major, in his first few months in office, then got into a terrible mess over his educational qualifications, at first refusing to disclose how many O levels he had and then testily admitting to 'some' gained by correspondence courses. Unlike Churchill and Callaghan (the only other non-graduate prime ministers since the war), he proved too obviously sensitive to the accusation that he was not up to the job owing to the fact that he was not a graduate.

This 'chippiness' is something he shares with Neil Kinnock. I was once told by someone who was part of the latter's entourage on the 1987 campaign that the only time he saw Kinnock speechless with rage was the morning he read an article in *The Times* accusing him of having an inferior intellect.

The public seems much less sensitive to this absence of degrees and other qualifications – the majority not having much more than a few GCSEs themselves. Sensibly they think intelligence can be proven by experience, not by qualifications alone, and that character is more important. It is certainly not worth falsifying one's educational records, as James Gulliver did (when he claimed in *Who's Who* to be a Harvard Business School MBA).

## War records

It used to be the fashion to embroider war records. In the 1828 presidential election, Andrew 'Old Hickory' Jackson ran on the slogan 'The Hero of Two Wars'. While he was indeed the victor at the Battle of New Orleans in 1815, his opponent somewhat acidly pointed out that in 1780 (during the War of Independence) Jackson was in fact only 13.

Kennedy certainly sailed close to the edge in his exploitation of the PT109 incident, but this was partly done to sidetrack the media away from his health problems (the cortical steroids he was taking gave his face a characteristic puffiness, the cause of which would have been obvious to any endocrinologist).

Johnson's accounts of his solitary experience of being under fire were also expanded beyond the bounds of truth, while both Harold Macmillan and Edward Heath were helped by their distinguished war records, as more recently Prince Andrew's Falklands service helped him modify the bread-roll throwing, hooray image he had previously conveyed.

Although George Bush's image makers assiduously publicized his Navy flier exploits in 1988, a 'good war' now seems to be fading as an integral part of a leader's image and, with the rise in prominence of women leaders, it somehow looks increasingly archaic and irrelevant.

Note that a criminal record is almost unheard of in this context, although Richard Branson has, until recently, managed to conceal his £8 fine for attempted poaching at the age of 18. Unluckily for him the US government ran a check and refused Virgin a liquor licence for seven years because of his Shakespearian misdemeanor.

## *Creed and colour*

Religious and ethnic background continue to contribute much to the image of leaders and the governing élite. The received wisdom over the water is that America is not ready for a presidential candidate 'whose name ends in a vowel', but that's what they said about a Catholic in the White House. Prior to Kennedy's bid for the vice presidential nomination at the 1956 convention, religion had not normally been an issue in US politics. Al Smith, a Catholic, had tried for the presidency in 1928 and had encountered prejudice, but he would have lost to Hoover even if he had been Episcopalian.

Adlai Stevenson's divorce hurt his image among Catholic voters in 1956, but this attitude faded during the 1960s and America finally elected its first divorced president in 1980.

Post-war, Jews who sought high office were often still considered beyond the pale, despite the fact that they had emerged in Wall Street and Hollywood as part of the industrial élite and that attitude applied even more strongly for negroes (as they were called then).

In the summer of 1960, Theodore Sorensen made the point to his colleagues that Kennedy would win if the 'religious issue' was neutralized. Indeed, given the percentage of voters in key states who were Catholic (eg New York, 40 per cent and Illinois, 30 per cent), his religion had the potential to be an actual advantage. The strategy adopted to defuse his Catholicism in the West Virginia primary was nothing less than masterly. Kennedy transformed the question of religion into a question of tolerance. As a result, when Humphrey (campaign song: *'Give me that Ol' Time Religion'*) raised it, he looked like a bigot. In his ads Kennedy emphasized that he would never go back on his oath of office by obedience to papal authority.

Nixon forbade his staff to make religion an issue, although the Republicans did get Al Smith's daughter to appeal to Catholic voters not to vote automatically for Kennedy just because of his religion. Finally Kennedy buried the issue by making what Kathleen Hall Jamieson regards as 'the most eloquent speech he made, either as candidate or president'. On 12 September 1960, less than two months before election day, he addressed the Greater Houston Ministerial Association in that city. He reminded his listeners of the religious freedoms Jefferson had introduced and the fact that religious toleration was the 'American Way', the America he fought for and his brother died for. He ended by quoting the presidential oath itself, emphasizing that, as a Catholic, he could not break such an oath to God and undermine the constitution. The speech was taped by his campaign's TV producer, Bill Wilson, and subsequently aired before his arrival in key Baptist-dominated cities, especially in the South.

By the 1980s, religion had faded as an issue to the extent that Reagan could use his ancestors – in Ballyporeen, Co Tipperary – as a useful opportunity for gaining favourable publicity.

In Britain, a Jew became a Tory prime minister in 1868 (although Disraeli was baptised a Protestant) and various shades of Non-conformism have also been represented at No 10.

Those with atheistic tendencies, if indeed there have been any, have either kept the information to themselves or, like Neil Kinnock, have covered the subject in a thick obfuscating layer of vagueness. Indeed, Kinnock once called Margaret Thatcher the 'Immaculate Mis-Conception'. I immediately sought and secured a response from the premier Catholic layman, the Duke of Norfolk, who fired off a stiff letter to *The Times* reflecting the Catholic community's outrage at such blasphemy. The row that followed seems to have cured him of making offensive religious remarks.

## *Sexuality*

As to sexual orientation, this is a subject that has become increasingly important in politics. In the US two congressmen have been re-elected (with increased majorities) even after it was revealed that they were homosexuals. In a recent New York City election three candidates stood: one (a lesbian) debating vociferously with another (who was HIV-positive) as to their respective qualifications for office. In some frustration, the third described himself as the 'dark-horse heterosexual candidate'.

In political Britain only Labour's treasury spokesman, Chris Smith, has revealed his homosexuality and this has not affected his promotion through Labour's ranks. In the Tory party, the whips' office know who is, but so far no one has admitted it.

In sport, it was not possible for Bill Tilden, the great Wimbledon champion of the 1930s, to 'come out' (indeed, he eventually went to prison after being convicted of homosexual offences), but Martina Navratilova's commercial career does not seem to have been damaged by her homosexuality (which is a contrast to Billie Jean King, who lost millions of dollars in advertising contracts).

In business, AT&T recently held a 'gay awareness week', while Lotus Computers now offer homosexual partners the same economic benefits as heterosexual spouses.

As image makers become public figures their own backgrounds are similarly coming under scrutiny. The Pentagon's spokesman during the Gulf War, Pete Williams, who became a familiar figure to television viewers, was moved by Dick Cheney soon afterwards to a lower profile job in the Pentagon when the media revealed his homosexual lifestyle. The explanation given for this was that homosexuality was illegal in the armed services of the US, so a double standard had to be avoided.

## *Wealth*

Wealth has always been a double-edged sword for the powerful, for it not only excites envy and accusations that power was bought and not earned, it also leads to charges that the rich are 'out of touch': electoral death to a modern politician or leader of industry. Post-war prime ministers have often had incomes other than their cabinet salaries, either by writing (Churchill, Wilson) or from family investments (Eden, Macmillan, Home, Thatcher).

US presidents have tended to be independently wealthy, L B Johnson heading the millionaires list. The nearest American voters got to choosing a small-town poor boy over a Harvard-educated, rich daddy's boy was Nixon vs Kennedy, but Nixon's image makers could never make the charge stick. Even a name can be used by the image makers to emphasize 'ordinariness'. Kennedy was always 'Jack', but Nixon was 'Richard' (except when Democrats called him 'Tricky Dicky'), *cf* 'Ted', 'Jim', 'Jerry', 'Jimmy', and 'Maggie'. (This last was, of course, never used by anyone truly close to the former prime minister; she has always been called Margaret by family and friends.)

While businesspeople in America are generally praised for the wealth they create for themselves and others, in Britain there is a constant sniping from the chattering classes, who both misquote and misunderstand the biblical aphorism that 'the *love* of money is the root of all evil'. There is some justice, however, in the criticisms of indefensibly huge salary increases awarded by non-executive directors to company managers of badly-run, unprofitable or near-monopoly organizations (one of whom recently obviously felt so guilty about receiving his 'bonus' that he immediately said he would give it to charity, thus emphasizing his own belief that he didn't deserve it).

All these background details are studied attentively by the media for clues. Consequently they are also used by image makers as a way of positioning their principals on ideological maps.

## *Family, fun and friends*

There are two other background factors that affect the way a member of the governing classes may be perceived, ie the people that surround them and their pastimes. Both of these 'humanize' a person, making them more accessible or friendly and therefore image makers tend to be inordinately fond of using these titbits of information to make the public feel they 'know' the person (yet another trick, incidentally, which they learnt from Hollywood).

There is nothing, however, more likely to strike terror into the image maker's heart than relatives of the principal. For every Denis Thatcher (nice, courteous, helpful and silent) there are two Billy Carters (drunken, loud, candid and available to the media). For every Jackie Kennedy (glamorous, supportive and useful) there is a Lady Howe, whose finest hour came when she tried to persuade her husband, Sir Geoffrey, to resign in protest at losing his job as foreign secretary on the night he became lord president of the council. For every Carol Thatcher (professional, objective, popular) there is a hapless Neal Bush involved in a financial scandal.

For some reason brothers seem particularly accident-prone. Kennedy had Teddy, while Johnson had to cover up the allegedly nefarious activities of his brother Sam. Nixon ordered the Secret Service to tail his brother Don and then put wire taps on his phones, all to make sure his business deals didn't backfire on the White House. Some leaders have actually appointed members of their family to jobs, eg Kennedy's appointment of Bobby (who had never tried a case in court) as attorney-general. In Britain, Callaghan appointed his son-in-law, Peter Jay, to be our ambassador in Washington. The announcement was accompanied by a Downing Street rubbishing of the incumbent, given to two reporters on the steps leading from the lobby room in the Commons. The evening papers both bore the same 'splash' – 'Snob Envoy Had to Go', which if anything gave even greater offence in Whitehall than the notion that the 'son-in-law also rises'. Nepotism is not particularly new, but it can be very damaging and is never worth the harm it does to a leader's reputation for fairness.

The press are fond of using relatives to 'get at' the powerful, eg Randolph Churchill, Nancy Reagan, Winnie Mandela, Mark Thatcher, Raisa Gorbachev, Rosalynn Carter and so on.

Cronies are even more dangerous than siblings, dragging the principal towards scandal and disgrace, eg Nixon/Rebozo, Carter/Lance, Wilson/Kagan etc.

Politicians often use their families for electoral reasons (for example, Heseltine's exploitation of his wife and children in the 1990 leadership contest), so the media rightly consider them fair game. The most ham-fisted and damaging case of this in recent times occurred when Carter revealed to a bemused nation in the 1980 Cleveland debate that he had asked his daughter Amy what the most 'important issue facing the nation' was. Her answer, 'the control of nuclear arms', sounded ridiculous on Carter's lips. The voters clearly felt that the president of the USA should be expected to figure out for himself what the most important issue facing the country he is supposed to be leading was, without recourse to a 13-year-old schoolgirl.

Families are not all downside, however. Eleanor Roosevelt was considered a major asset to her husband's career. Barbara Bush is, as I write, the most popular woman in America. The Princess of Wales is universally loved and admired by the British people, thereby improving the image of the royal family – although she has a double-edged, if unintentional, effect of sometimes making her husband look more old-fogeyish than he really is.

Outside of family and friends, the 'private' lives of the powerful are fertile ground for the image maker. The people they entertain and honour is a very fruitful area. Pierre Salinger, Kennedy's press secretary, was very conscious of the potential for building the 'Camelot' image by using 'court' musicians like Casals, Copland and Bernstein. Wilson was quick to see the benefit of awarding the Beatles MBEs, thus reinforcing the positioning as a modernist, populist government he had developed in 1963–4. His receptions at No 10 overflowed with actors, footballers, comedians, pop stars and others from that entertaining, if sometimes louche, fantasy world, 'swinging London' (itself a media invention of *Time* magazine).

The tabloids in particular love a good 'Gazza meets Maggie' photograph and, when both subjects are as famous as this pairing, then even the Birtiste BBC is not above including the pictures on the *Nine O'Clock News*.

Image is not based on abstract notions (as some journalists at the posher end of the media think), but on small but revealing facts about the person (or company, brand etc) involved. Take pets, for example. They serve a useful function in normalizing the powerful. We know that the Queen loves horses and corgis. Churchill dearly loved his poodle, Rufus; while his budgie, Toby, habitually perched on a sponge atop the prime minister's head as he worked on boxes. A previous generation grew to share Roosevelt's love for his dog Fala and then sympathize with Checkers, Nixon's pet. Baldwin liked to be photographed scratching the back of a pig, for all the world as if he was the owner of Blandings Castle. Chamberlain, his somewhat austere successor, was made a little bit more human by revealing the fact that he was a keen bird-watcher.

When Margaret Thatcher's talented image maker, Christine Wall, wanted to portray a prime minister relaxing on holiday in Cornwall in 1986, she borrowed 'Polo', a King Charles spaniel, and had Mrs T photographed being energetically dragged by the diminutive dog along the local beach. The prime minister's unnecessarily Stakhanovite image was thus softened considerably.

Those, like me, who find it possible to forgive almost anything of anyone who loves horses, watched entranced at Reagan's relaxed hacking over the Californian countryside, but Johnson shocked America when he held his beagles up by their ears (normal practice in rural Texas). Animals humanize – odd but true.

Hobbies likewise. James Hagerty, Eisenhower's press secretary, encouraged pictures of the president painting, as he was an accomplished portrait artist. When I was asked, at the 1991 secret strategy meeting at Hever Castle, to recommend a plan for John Major's photo opportunities, I suggested that, as he was the youngest prime minister since Rosebery, sport should be the theme. I pointed out that it is hard to make politics relevant to young people's lives, but if they could see pictures of a prime minister in the stands during soccer and cricket matches (Saturdays only), then they might come to the conclusion that this might be someone who understood their hopes and fears.

Churchill took up the relaxed-looking hobby of bricklaying, cheekily applying to join the appropriate union, while George Bush throws horseshoes, which in the States is a 'bloke-ish' kind of hobby. This, as well as his liking for fishing (and eating pork rinds), is often used in evidence that his other 'rich man' hobbies, like power-boat racing, are mere aberrations.

The most concerted effort to use sport for image-making purposes was in the Heath era. Worried that his bachelor status and musical interests gave him a less than macho persona, his sailing activities were deliberately given very wide publicity. In fact the electorate was looking for the 'smack of real government', not success in the Sydney to Hobart race. In my view this is a good example of trying to fix something that was never really broken and, in doing so, giving the principal a falsely macho (and élitist) image that crumbled to dust when, in 1972, Heath reneged on his policies and U-turned. In my experience the best principle to follow is always to exploit a strength, rather than try to remedy a weakness.

## The influence of personality

All of these background details can be used by image makers to make leaders less remote; they make it harder for leaders' opponents to accuse them of being out of touch with the average person's concerns. They also provide part of that library of information that helps the viewer to judge the leader's personality. No one will ever be able to define the exact importance of personality, but common sense tells us that it has an important influence. Indeed, Sir Bernard Ingham (Mrs Thatcher's chief press secretary from 1979–90) once went so far as to suggest that 'politics is about personalities'.

The primary interest for the image maker in this area is the constant search for ways of dramatizing aspects of personality that are on the face of it intangible. Speakers can borrow wit, charm, learning, wisdom and truth from others. Cunning can be learnt, as can hard work and consistency. How, however, can conviction, optimism, determination or honesty be communicated? Most difficult of all, how can caring and competence be brought alive? Moreover, can these be faked?

One should distinguish first between manner or temperament and personality. The former can be both modified or concealed by the image makers, if it is necessary to do this. A distant or hesitant manner can be improved, while a short temper can be concealed, at least on a temporary basis. A nervous temperament can be soothed and vanity discreetly discouraged. However, no image maker can do other than accept the basic *character* of their principal. Character is formed long before image makers get their hands on them, and it cannot be greatly altered or hidden.

In 1968 a survey was carried out among voters, who were asked 'What are the most important qualities needed for running the country well?'. They listed the following adjectives (in priority order): 'straightforward', 'hardworking', 'sincere', 'strong' and 'confident'. 'Likeable', 'kindly' and 'unassuming' were included at the bottom of the list. When asked which of these was most likely to be revealed by television, they said confidence and sincerity. While these respondents were right to feel that television can 'reveal' character, I'm not so sure that it applies to all.

Take two 'star' performers of recent times, Harolds Macmillan and Wilson. The legends of Supermac's unflappability are told and re-told. When interrupted by Khrushchev banging his shoe on his desk during Macmillan's 1960 UN speech, he stopped and asked quietly, 'Mr President, perhaps we could have a translation. I could not quite follow.' (It was only afterwards that someone noticed that Khrushchev was still wearing *both* his shoes.) When he sacked one-third of his cabinet colleagues in the 'night of the long knives' reshuffle, he passed it off insouciantly as 'a little local difficulty'. In fact he was an extremely highly strung, sensitive man who was often physically sick before prime minister's questions. To conceal this he 'wore the mask' of patrician disdain, mixed with carefully manufactured calm.

The other Harold was a great fan of his predecessor and copied the pre-planned 'ad libs' Macmillan was so fond of. In Wilson's case it was the real thing, but the 'sincerity' that television recorded concealed a Machiavellian personality. In both cases, television (at least at first) never pierced their armour-plating, although it must be admitted that these two were quite exceptional performers.

The debate over how much personality plays a part in gaining power is one that fascinates the media. Psephologists, in their usual spoil-sport fashion, say personality matters, but not as much as the media believe. They cite polling carried out in the pre-election years to prove that sometimes the less popular leader won. In the last six elections the popularity figures were as follows: 1970 – Wilson 51 per cent/Heath 28 per cent; 1974 (February) – Heath 38 per cent/Wilson 38 per cent; 1974 (October) – Wilson 45 per cent/Heath 43 per cent; 1979 – Callaghan 43 per cent/Thatcher 43 per cent; 1983 – Thatcher 48 per cent/Foot 17 per cent; 1987 – Thatcher 41 per cent/Kinnock 45 per cent. From this we can infer that it is at least possible to win an election without being the most popular leader.

In my view the leader's personality in non-presidential politics like Britain's has rarely been critical, but it has occasionally been important. It may well be very significant in close-fought elections among those who have weak party loyalties. These floating voters need to know whether they can trust the party's promises, and the best way they have to judge this (apart from the record) is to assess the sincerity of the leaders. Television increases this focus because its hunger for pictures makes it concentrate on people, not words, although we should not forget that the average voter can't even recognize most senior politicians when shown a photograph of them.

The pull of party is still stronger in the voting booth than the attraction of leaders' personalities, even when the parties' policies converge, as is now the case post-Thatcher. John Major's popularity may well count in a 1992 election, especially if it is a close-run thing, but it didn't improve his party's 1991 ratings, mired as they were in economic gloom. If it does count, it will be because he fits with the *zeitgeist*. As John Hanvey (the chairman of Harris Research) says, mere popularity is not enough, 'it is much more important that the leader chimes with people's values and the mood of the time'. Major's background is a good fit with a society looking to extend opportunities to all and that is why he is an asset to the Tory party (and not because he is a likeable, decent and honest chap – that is simply a bonus).

Most successful politicians are gifted actors whose performance both counts and, to an extent, conceals. The secret of getting it right lies in the maxim crisply expressed by John

Hegarty (one of the most talented advertising experts of my generation) as 'Be yourself, but not too much'. For example, Neil Kinnock is naturally verbose and, if he were really true to himself, he presumably would not bother to contain his natural inclination to use a dozen words when one or two would do. In fact he rightly strains not to be too 'natural' and has proved much more effective at prime minister's questions because of it. Sir Bernard Ingham is doubtful that much can be done to hide defects, observing that 'you are what you are. You may try and hide your principal's shortcomings, but in the end they will emerge'. Ingham feels that the great danger of emphasizing the importance of personality PR is that 'people will believe that you can make someone into something they are not, when it isn't true'.

There is another danger in overemphasis on personality: it can lead to the principal becoming too bland. Leaders in any field need an edge of conviction and enthusiasm in their voice and manner in order to convey credibility. If you over-sanitize them, you normalize them, and that feeling of specialness disappears. The viewer loses the sense of the person's individuality, without which it is difficult to trust someone completely.

Mrs Thatcher was remarkably well served in this respect by her image makers, in two regards. First, they never tried to persuade the British public that they should like her, only that they should respect her, even when the former might have seemed much more to her electoral advantage. Secondly, they accurately identified her strengths: courage, conviction and vision, then single-mindedly underlined them.

By contrast, Neil Kinnock has been let down by his image makers on occasion because of their lack of faith in him. He has been changed by them from being a man driven by a particular vision of the way government should exercise its powers to being a managed man, seemingly reneging on the socialist principles he adopted and espoused with such vigour throughout his early years as an MP. When he weakly allowed his CND membership to 'lapse', it may be reassuring for a few (probably implacably Tory) voters to know, but it also made him look inconsistent – which in the long run is much more damaging.

To be a leader it is necessary both to have vision and yet retain Rudyard Kipling's 'common touch'. The latter can, of course, be manufactured. The British Army, for example, does so when it teaches Sandhurst cadets that 'the men eat before the officers'. It is also institutionalized in the Roman Catholic Church, as when at Easter the Pope washes the feet of 12 people in remembrance of Christ's humility at the Last Supper.

When returning from his inaugural, Jimmy Carter leaned forward, told his Secret Service bodyguard to stop the car and stepped out on to Pennsylvania Avenue. At first the crowds were puzzled, thinking something was wrong with the car, and then it dawned on them: 'They're walking', Carter heard them gasp. As he reveals in his memoirs, he had planned this, to demonstrate, he said, confidence in the people and deliberately to reduce the status of the president and of his family. It was probably the finest moment of his presidency. So often power does not corrupt, so much as distance from reality. The powerful start to believe they are immortal or have ju-ju powers or are men of destiny or some such nonsense. They find it increasingly hard to be objective about themselves and a corrosive vanity often sets in. Lyndon Johnson, for example, loved to drive at 120mph in his Lincoln convertible. One day a Texas state trooper stopped him for speeding. The cop looked in the window and in shock exclaimed 'Oh my God Almighty!' Johnson looked at him squarely and said 'And don't you forget it'. Those who retain the common touch are forgiven much. When Monty visited his troops he would always hand out drums of cigarettes, despite that fact he hated cigarette smoke. A simple ploy, but one that successfully reminded his men that he cared for their welfare.

Tiny touches like this one are surprisingly effective. The habit top American managers have of always repeating your name when you are introduced helps them remember it on next meeting. I remember talking to Kelvin McKenzie, the ebullient editor of the *Sun*, some years ago and questioning him closely on his opinion of Margaret Thatcher. After a conventional account of her sterling qualities, he suddenly turned to me and said that the thing that had really impressed him was that, on the second occasion they met, the prime minister remembered McKenzie's wife's occupation. From little acorns such as these chance remarks do *Sun* endorsements grow.

Vision, on the other hand, is impossible to fake because it is extremely hard to maintain the impression that you have it when under pressure. As Kenneth Baker says, 'A good image has to spring from a deep well and not a shallow stream.' He goes on: 'Unless you have a coherent set of beliefs from which policy derives, then I don't think you will be a successful politician. If it is just a question of presentation, eventually you'll be found out.' Leaders who have a consistent set of principles and values are extremely rare, at least in government, although in business they are much more common: eg Thomas Alva Edison, Ray Kroc, Akio Morita, Kemmons Wilson, Thomas J Watson and Forrest Mars. Vision can, it seems, be inherited. In the early 1980s I once attended a meeting in New York concerning the then arcane subject of brand globalization with Mars' son, Forrest Jnr. One puzzled executive asked him why he was spending so much time and money on this, when he would never see any return in his lifetime. 'I am not doing it for me,' Mars said. 'I am doing it for my grandchildren.' Now that's what I call vision.

In post-war politics, Charles de Gaulle, Martin Luther King and Margaret Thatcher stand out for their conviction and for their single-mindedness. It takes great courage to be this different yet this certain. Politicians in Britain, who may be tempted to follow these visionaries, have before them the careers of both Sir Keith Joseph and Enoch Powell, both men of vision, both smashed by a single speech ('pills for proles' and 'rivers of blood' respectively). It is a very brave leader who challenges the shibboleths of the time – the rewards may be great, but equally the humiliation can be complete.

It is important for image makers not only to discover *what* someone believes in, but also *why* they believe it, because it is much easier to communicate an idea if it can be personalized. For example, Margaret Thatcher believed passionately in opportunity for all but we were plagued with the problem of how to communicate the basis for this passion. The intellectual case is impeccable but cold. The patriotic case (wanting your country to become stronger by using all the talent available) is sound, but could come across as a little high-falutin'. One evening, before going in to dinner in the small dining room at No 10, I was standing chatting with the prime minister and Dr Richard Wirthlin and the conversation turned to our respective social backgrounds. (Respectively, Durham miner's grandson, grocer's daughter and Mormon Bishop's son.) Hearing Mrs

Thatcher talk about hers, I suddenly realized how to approach the problem. What people needed to hear was that she still remembered her struggle to achieve something in life, and that she had not forgotten what it was like to look up the class mountain, rather than surveying the world from the peaks and ridges of comfortable middle-class England.

From that moment on, I badgered all and sundry to include a passage in her next speech referring to her Grantham roots. The result was one of the most effective of her later speeches, made at Cheltenham on the 31 March, 1990.

As she came off the stage, I could see she was pleased, and told her that the 'back to the roots' part had worked well. Next day the press agreed.

The *Sunday Times*, under the headline 'Thatcher whips up Tory fervour', summarized her speech perfectly: 'With all the self-assurance which has seen her through difficult times before', Michael Jones wrote, 'she recalled her roots, her father, the kind of people she grew up with and had become party leader to defend, and said she shared their hopes and worries. They did not expect the moon. What they wanted were more ordinary things, the things she wanted, too.'

Reagan's principles were also based on experience rather than pure reason. In 1949 he spent four months in England filming *The Hasty Heart* and saw first-hand how the welfare state had already sapped the people's incentive to work. Reagan was *au fond* a Jeffersonian Democrat (he campaigned for Truman in 1948 and against Nixon in the 1950 Senate race), who idolized Roosevelt and was much influenced by his alcoholic, shoe salesman father, Jack (who was an active Democrat). Reagan quotes Jefferson on the legitimate concerns of good government approvingly in his memoirs. 'A wise and frugal government,' Jefferson said, 'which shall restrain men from injuring one another, shall leave them otherwise free to regulate their own pursuits of industry and of improvement and shall not take from the mouth of labour the bread it has earned – this is the sum of good government.'

Reagan came to realize that the left had moved away from their instinctive anti-government stance, bringing the danger of (as James Madison once put it) 'an abridgement of the freedom of the people by gradual and silent encroachment of those in power'. His speechwriters, especially Peggy Noonan, never forgot *why* Reagan constantly emphasized the individual's rights: it was because he still carried with him the emotional shock of finding out that the ends he sought had been perverted by the means the left had chosen to employ.

The most important leadership quality – courage – is beyond image making. When the royal family visits leper colonies (as the Queen did on her 1956 trip to Nigeria) or AIDS patients (as the Princess of Wales has repeatedly done), they rightly excite our admiration and respect. Churchill's courage in 1940 stands out even in his long career in public life. Kennedy's courage to face crippling back pain or John Wakeham's daily agony following the Brighton bomb indicate an inner core of rare strength. Yeltsin's brute courage in facing down tanks or Dubcek's stand against the same coarse, drunken bullies in 1968, encourages us all that might is not always right or even inevitable.

Probably the most emotional moment of my time in Central Office came when the democratic leaders of Hungary, Poland and Czechoslovakia assembled in Bournemouth to thank Mrs Thatcher for helping them throw off the shackles of communism. The stolid, ordinary Britons in the audience stood, applauding wildly; many cried as they cheered. Some of the speakers had been tortured, others imprisoned or exiled. All of them were living witness that mankind cannot be bound in the state's chain's for ever: sooner or later it will break free. I doubt there was a person in that place who didn't ask themselves the same question: 'Would *I* have had the courage these people had, to speak out for freedom and justice?'. Hopefully that is a question we will never be forced to answer in Britain.

One last story. When Khrushchev first visited America he attended a press conference at the Washington Press Club. The very first question was, 'Today you talked about the hideous rule of your predecessor, Stalin. You were one of his closest aides and colleagues during those years. What were *you* doing all that time?'. By the time the interpreter had finished, Khrushchev was in a rage. 'Who asked that?', he shouted. All 500 reporters studied their shoelaces. 'Who asked that?', he repeated. Silence. '*That's* what I was doing,' Khrushchev said.

# 3

# The Marketing of Power

Hail to BBDO,
it told the nation how to go.
It managed by advertisement,
to sell us a new President.
Philip Morris, Lucky Strike,
Alka-Seltzer, I like Ike.

*Marya Mannes.*

This chapter is concerned with the use of modern marketing techniques in the struggle to gain power. It deals with the use of market research, positioning theory, advertising, direct marketing, stage-managed meetings, design and brand association techniques. Note, not marketing itself, which hardly exists in politics. Politicians do not ask the voters what they want; they only seek reactions from the voter to what they have already decided to do.

Most of these methods were developed by American multinationals and were modified by their admen, who then fed them through to the politicians. Whereas American politicians, often being former businesspeople, understood very quickly the potential of these ideas, a combination of the ivory tower backgrounds and anti-business bias (not solely a preserve of the left) of their British counterparts often combined to produce a fundamental misunderstanding of their potential. A basic (sometimes wilful) ignorance of marketing theory and advertising practice means that one still hears daft comments like 'they are trying to sell parties as if they were soap powder'. Any marketer knows, first, that it is the seriousness of a brand choice that determines the approach and, secondly, that the extent to which the choices are differentiated is what determines the complexity of the marketing process. The casual choice of commodities (like soap powder) does not therefore produce many parallels with the choice of a governing party nor lessons for political advertising.

The key contribution that marketing advisers have made to the political process is to adapt their techniques and modes of thinking to the process of persuasion.

First, they introduced politicians to the benefits of sound market research and this, as we shall see, has changed the way policy is presented. They then persuaded their masters to think strategically instead of tactically, by introducing such marketing concepts as positioning theory, and insisted that the discipline of strategy driving execution should be upheld. Finally, they brought new executional techniques like negative advertising and direct marketing into campaigning.

## The effect of research

At first market research for political purposes consisted of recording voting intentions and voters' attitudes to lists of 'issues', ie policy areas such as the economy, health, education, defence and so on. The problem with this type of opinion polling is that the electorate has learnt to use voting intention questions in much the same way as they use by-elections or local government elections, to box the government's ears for various imagined misdemeanours and failures. They do this, however, safe in the knowledge that anything they say or do, or any way they vote, is not going to bring the government down. It is a risk-free and highly satisfying strategy. However, when a general election looms, the electorate reverts back to using a quite different *modus operandum*. Minds are concentrated and simple, yet vitally important questions are asked, eg who will increase my family's standard of living and their quality of life? It is at this point that the electorate is most susceptible to the persuasive techniques of the image makers.

Until 1980 no one had found a convincing research method that could tap into this thought process and use it to influence the choice of party or leader in the run-up to an election. The Thatcher and Reagan victories of 1979/80 proved a watershed in the use of market research to gain power. In both cases research was extensively used to understand the voter better and isolate discrete target groups; the core beliefs of the two parties were correctly identified and brief, clear positioning strategies created; finally these strategies were expertly executed by properly funded advertising and direct marketing campaigns.

It all started in 1952, when a Chicago University professor named David Riesman wrote a book called *The Lonely Crowd*. This one volume revolutionized the nature and scope of political research in the 1980s. Riesman analyzed the way in which certain 'social character' types are deployed in the work, play and child-rearing activities of adult life. Riesman identified three different groupings: tradition-directed, inner-directed and other-directed. Each group, he claimed, was dominant in certain periods of history, and in societies that he characterized respectively as fixed, transitional and declining (echoes of Marx's thesis, antithesis, synthesis).

The 'inner-directed' group, Riesman said, all have one thing in common, ie the source of direction for the individual is 'inner' in the sense that it is implanted early in life by their elders and directed toward generalized, but none the less inescapably destined, goals. The 'other-directed' group's source of direction comes from contemporaries, friends and the mass media (what the sociologists call 'peer groups').

For the first time those in the communication business were given a way of dividing up their audience, not by demographics like age, gender, occupation, income etc, but by *psychographics* like social, religious and cultural values. Riesman's work was later expanded by the Stanford Research Institute (in their *Values and Lifestyles* studies), who finally ended up with the eight categories they named: 'Strugglers, Believers, Strivers, Makers, Fulfilled, Achievers, Experiencers and Actualizers'. This new idea was quickly picked up by the ad men, as they will pick up (and then drop) any shiny new toy that comes their way. Ludicrous attempts were then made to sell consumer products like baked beans by reference to important and deeply held values.

However, one group of market researchers started to take this social/psychological taxonomy very seriously indeed, and these were the research advisers to political parties. This was because the voter's choice of parties, unlike the choice of which brand of baked beans to buy, is driven by the self-same values that Riesman had been discussing.

In politics it is relatively easy to discover which issues the voters think are important at any one point in time. It is more difficult to ascertain accurately what depth of importance each issue has for each voter. It is very difficult indeed to discover why these issues are important in the first place. As the relative importance of issues changes all the time, planning a communication strategy can sometimes resemble trying to fire a rifle at a moving target which is shrouded in fog. If, therefore, a way could be found to get behind the issues of the day and discover the reasons why voters held the attitudes they did, this fog might be dispersed. Put simply, issues change, values don't.

It was at this point that Dr Richard Wirthlin entered the picture. Dick Wirthlin is a practising Mormon, who was formerly a professor at Brigham Young University and an econometrics expert. He first met Reagan in 1969 when the future president was governor of California, but it wasn't until 1974 that he started advising him on a regular basis. By the end of the 1970s only 28 per cent of the US electorate considered themselves Republicans, but Wirthlin felt Reagan could become president if he based his appeal (through his choice of issues, his policy ideas and his personality) on the values that were deeply held by Democrats and Independents, in much the same way that Mrs Thatcher, though never very 'popular' in the orthodox sense, successfully appealed to Labour voters by holding the same (mainly traditional) values as they did.

The methodology Wirthlin used to discover these values was relatively simple, and is still highly secret, but in essence, voters were encouraged in interviews to express their feelings about what was important to them in their daily lives and the reasons for this importance.

From this data it was possible to draw a line directly from the values that the voters held, to the issues that were important to them. Wirthlin then advised Reagan that if he could tap into the enduring values and issues connected with 'family, neighbour-hood, workplace, peace and freedom', then the resultant image could overcome the ancient tribal loyalties that would otherwise give the South to Carter. He was exactly right. Theodore White later called Wirthlin's 176-page campaign plan 'black book' 'one of the major political documents of our time'. This research created the strategy that inspired the Reagan *This is a Man* 'bio-pic' film that proved so extraordinarily successful. In attracting support from Democrats, this mini-documentary is one of the most significant pieces of political communication of modern times, copied by many US politicians (and one British leader) but never bettered. Reagan, the film's voice-over said, was raised 'in America's heartland, small-town Illinois. He gained from his close-knit family, a sense for the values of the family, even though luxuries were few and hard to come by.' In Hollywood his appeal 'came from his roots, his character' and 'he appealed to audiences because he was so clearly one of them'. Reagan's service record (since disputed) during the Second World War and his presidency of the Screen Actor's Guild were also cited as evidence of his patriotic and leadership values. His record as governor of California – 'he saved the state from bankruptcy' – emphasized his qualities of competence and strength of purpose.

## Values research

For the image makers this concept of values research represents a quantum leap in constructing communication strategies. To return to the UK context, it becomes blindingly obvious, with the help of this type of research, that the value motivating attitudes to the NHS is 'a sense of security', a need for peace of mind, especially as we grow older, hence the depth of opposition to any hint of privatization plans, which are perceived as an attempt to exclude working people from receiving a high quality service.

As for education, it becomes equally obvious that this issue is driven by the voters' belief in and desire for an 'opportunity' society. If education is presented as the prime mechanism of a meritocracy then, whatever the policy, it is likely to be accepted. If education policies are seen as élitist, then it becomes unlikely that parents will ever accept them. Both the language and the symbols of these values can therefore be used in, for example, speeches and advertising to drive the benefits of policy home. The only exceptions to this general theorizing are religious and patriotic values, as overt use of their symbols is easily detectable and can make the communication clumsy and obvious.

## The poll tax – accountability or fairness?

A classic example of getting the values associated with the issue wrong, was the British Government's campaign for the launch of the poll tax. The government's chosen battleground was the benefit of accountability that the new tax would bring. In fact, this was far too arcane a concept to be easily grasped. The campaign should have single-mindedly centred on the value of 'fairness', ie everyone should pay for what they use.

No tax is ever going to be popular but, by not addressing the fairness issue properly, a predictably unpopular smoothing out of the local taxation burden, turned into an occasion for rioting, civil disobedience and eventually, through the panic of a few political pygmies, it caused the downfall of Mrs Thatcher (divisions over Europe acted only as the shot at Sarajevo did). The real reason for the coup was the belief (backed by opinion polls) among backbench MPs in marginal seats that a) the level of the poll tax compared with the rates would endanger their seats and b) Mrs Thatcher would neither abolish the tax nor reduce its level by subsidy. She could have stayed in office by promising them either of these and, what's more, she knew it.

Wirthlin's research methodology represents the most important advance in political communications of the last two decades. It provides the image makers with the best possible guide to the effective presentation of policy, by creating a clear understanding of how voters make their choice of party. It also supplies them with a rich and subtle vocabulary of persuasive language and motivating symbols. The party that first grasps the true importance of Wirthlin's work and applies it to the British political process will win an enormous advantage over their opponents and greatly increase their chances of gaining power.

## Positioning the brand

All effective communication strategies contain what is called a positioning statement, a clear analysis of *what* the brand (or company, person, political party etc) is for: *who* it is for, and *why* anyone should be interested in choosing it.

## What *is it for?*

The first of these is much harder to get right than it seems at first sight and in both politics and business, this is where most of the image makers' time is spent, much more than in executional techniques such as advertising. The process starts with a definition of the functional and psychological benefits of the brand.

Every product or service has a functional benefit which meets a basic need. Food gives nourishment, clothes provide warmth, houses shelter us, cars get us from A to B and so on. They also each have a psychological benefit which meets a basic want. Sevruga Caviare fulfils a want for luxurious self-indulgence; *haute couture* a desire for individuality or prestige; a Rolls-Royce a desire to be admired.

The psychological benefit is normally much the most important aspect of many brands, as the functional value is often only the evidence that the promise of the psychological benefit is credible. The fact that a Ferrari Testarossa accelerates from 0–60 in 5.8 seconds (which in marketing jargon is called a 'feature') is but supporting evidence of the proposition that the car is the most exciting, impressive and glamorous object on four wheels that money can buy. It is true and relevant, but it isn't why anyone would pay £123,119 for the red beast.

Functional benefits are often confused with features, especially in politics, where the distinction between a feature (an aspect of technical performance or an ingredient) and the benefit to the consumer is still rarely understood. As Sir Tim Bell rightly observes, 'the biggest problem with advising politicians about communications is that (with the honourable exception of Mrs Thatcher) they cannot seem to grasp the difference between information and persuasion'. One of the most important consequences of using marketing advisers in post-war politics is their insistence on the primacy of benefits over features. Each piece of legislation comprises a list of features, but it is the effective communication of its prime benefit that will attract the voters' approval. Two examples from policy initiatives should suffice to illustrate the point.

### The 'benefits' of legislation

The Social Security Act 1986 introduced the Family Credit Scheme. The main *feature* of this system was that payments would be made to working families on low incomes, so that they would find it financially worth their while to seek employment. The *benefits* to recipients in terms of both their self-esteem and the family's standard of living (and quality of life) were what made the scheme popular.

The Education Reform Act 1988 introduced the concept of the national curriculum. The principal *feature* of this system was that all children would study ten foundation subjects. The *benefit* was that children would be better equipped to live and work in the world after school, improving both the range of employment opportunities they could aspire to and their ability to handle the challenges that these opportunities would bring.

The benefits that derive from legislative features are not always obvious to the voter without clear exposition. Features on their own mostly seem irrelevant or simply mystifying. It is vital, therefore, that any political party should be clear how its promised policies should improve the everyday life of the voter and ensure that these benefits, when identified, are related to the core values of the party.

### Number 2 brands

There are two key factors that affect brand positioning: a change in the environment that surrounds the brand, and the brand's position within the market universe. One of the most difficult marketing problems to solve is the positioning of 'Number 2' brands. The quality usually has to be as good as that of the brand leader, but it is difficult to command the same price and therefore the profit margin is often considerably lower. This inhibits investment in the brand and therefore its chances of overtaking the brand leader. Brand leaders often have become so by adopting the generic benefit of the market ('Persil washes whiter', 'Nothing acts faster than Anadin'), and the Number 2 often struggles for a *raison d'être* other than value (which the brand leader, with superior economies of scale, can usually deliver better).

In politics this problem is made more complicated by the fact that our first-past-the-post voting system means that the winner scoops the pot, leaving the Number 2 with little or nothing.

As Robin Wight (of the WCRS advertising agency and former advertising consultant to the Tory party) has pointed out, the strategies used by consumer brand leaders and challengers have great relevance to politics. In 1988 George Bush was clearly seen as what marketing people call a 'line extension' to President Reagan, while Governor Michael Dukakis of Massachusetts was positioned by his image makers as a line extension of a liberal Democrat tradition extending back to F D Roosevelt. The Bush team, being 17 points behind in the early stages of the election campaign, decided to try and force Governor Dukakis off this positioning by concentrating their attacks on what they called the 'L-word', ie liberalism. Every effort was made to portray the core values of the Democrats as synonymous with tax and spend, welfare hand-outs and 1960s permissiveness. Partly encouraged by his poll ratings and partly out of a panic reaction to these attacks, the Dukakis team started the process of moving away from their challenger strategy to a brand leader image of presidential proportions, emphasizing professionalism and competence. (There is a wise old saw in US Presidential politics that if you run a Republican against a Republican, the Republican always wins. Substitute the word Conservative and it's just as valid in the UK. Dukakis was posing as a Republican, as Kinnock sometimes poses as a Conservative.)

The delighted Republican team, led by the nearest thing to an attack Doberman in human form, Lee Atwater, and the most experienced political advertising expert in the US, Roger Ailes, went for the challenger. Ridiculing him as 'Zorba the Clerk', they attacked his competence, using as evidence the pollution of Boston harbour and the policy of giving prisoners leave while still serving out their sentences. The *soi-disant* 'president' was quickly perceived for what he was: an averagely competent, middle-manager type, whose only experience of running anything was a middle-ranking Eastern seaboard state.

Voters were then invited to make a comparison with (given Reagan's clear endorsement) his opponent's professional qualifications. George Bush had been UN ambassador and chairman of the Republican National Committee, as well as director of the CIA and vice-president for eight years. Any marketing consultant could have predicted what happened next: Dukakis was buried. So strong was the vice-president's position that it even survived the adoption of Quayle as running mate, and the latter's destruction by Senator Lloyd Bentsen in the Omaha debate. Remember? *Quayle* [defensively] 'I have as much congressional experience as Senator John Kennedy had when he became president.' *Bentsen* [drily] 'Jack Kennedy was a friend of mine, and Senator, you're no Jack Kennedy.'

*Line extensions*

The 1988 'more of the same' US election makes an interesting contrast with the 1976 Ford–Carter race or the 1964 Home–Wilson election. In both cases the incumbent was a line extension of an unsuitable predecessor. By pardoning Nixon, Ford put himself into the camp of the Watergate conspirators. The fact that this was an act of great courage (as he knew perfectly well what the consequences would be) did not save him at the polls. Carter – who had even less relevant experience than Dukakis – positioned himself as the classic challenger, in this version as 'anti-Washington', meaning opposed to the cynicism and amorality of the Nixon White House.

In 1964 Harold Wilson positioned himself as both firmly in the traditions of democratic socialism and as the champion of the new technology whose 'white heat' would sweep away a tired, aristocratic, scandal-prone government. The Tory party magic circle's choice of Sir Alec Douglas-Home proved fatal; their only hope had been in choosing someone who was not seen as a line extension of '13 years of misrule' by grouse-moor Tories. Given the closeness of the result it seems at least possible that a modernist leader like Macleod could have survived Labour's onslaught by attracting the votes that went to the Liberals.

In 1979 Mrs Thatcher, advised by marketing men like Tim Bell, adopted a traditional challenger strategy. She did not pretend that she was as experienced as Callaghan, although she provided enough reassurance for it not to be an issue. Instead she charged Callaghan's administration with presiding over

Britain's decline into a third-rate, off-shore aircraft carrier, with an over-taxed, over-governed and demoralized workforce ordered about by antediluvian trade union bosses. She promised to set the people free and give them back control over their lives. The 'Winter of Discontent' did the rest.

The opportunity for a Labour leader to win in 1992 has been based on an identical analysis. A determined campaign based on the need for a change after '13 wasted years', would see votes haemorrhaging to both opposition parties, especially if Labour could also reassure the voters that public services would improve – without tax increases.

*Developing new products*

In business one of the most important uses of core brand values analysis is in the development of new products. It is obviously cheaper to use an existing brand name, rather than invest the huge sums of money needed to achieve the kind of brand name awareness that is a *sine qua non* of success. Clearly, Cadbury Bath Cleaner and Flash Dairy Assortment are not going to work, but vice versa might.

In politics the calculations are more complex. John Major is not seeking to become a 'line extension' of Mrs Thatcher, but rather of the party she led for 15 years. He needs, therefore, to define exactly what that party now stands for and define how much of those core values are in fact the result of that long leadership. He might, like her, conclude that the party stood for liberty and prosperity, but that his tactics for achieving these twin strategic objectives may be somewhat different from his predecessor's. In that case he need not worry too much over small differences between them. If the voters want liberty and prosperity, and understand that he promises both, and believe that they are more likely to obtain both from his party than any other, then they will follow his election parade into the voting booth.

Neil Kinnock's party was forced into repositioning by means of a policy review. Out went the previous 'equality and peace' positioning and in came 'opportunity and caring'. The credibility of the latter is not an issue, but he is evidently struggling to substantiate the former.

[91]

This 'competence and caring' strategic see-saw has dominated politics here and in the US since the Depression. In 1945 the nation chose 'caring', and kicked its 'competent' leader out. In 1979, tired of endless incompetence, they kicked out a popular incumbent. In general, the more effective way to become brand leader in Britain is to emphasize one value (preferably competence) and reassure the voter that the other (caring) exists in sufficient depth. The result of most elections thereby hangs on either a desire to get rid of a government (eg 1945, 1964, 1979) or confirm the incumbent on the basis that the opposition is unacceptable (eg 1959, 1983). This means that under normal circumstances there are only two effective communications strategies, both of which are based on a balance of competence, caring and amount of change from the past. These may be characterized as the brand leader's 'we've achieved something and the other lot will ruin it' and the challenger strategy, 'they have been given every chance to achieve something and look at the mess they've made'. Examples are: 'Life's better with the Conservatives. Don't let Labour ruin it' from the 1959 election and 'Let's make America great again' from the Reagan–Bush 1980 campaign.

*Sticking to your positioning*

Having confirmed or discovered a suitable positioning, the hardest problem is sticking to it, while at the same time looking to improve it. All advertising executives are familiar with the consequences of personnel changes at the top of client companies. Time and time again the decline of brands is due to a 'new broom' arriving and deciding that the brand's positioning is no longer 'relevant'. In my experience there is no advertising idea so successful that some ambitious whizz kid won't try and get rid of it.

Here is a typical example of the problem. A few years ago I was lunching with the industrialist Asil Nadir in a (vain) attempt to extract money from him for Tory party funds. Naturally enough I was trying to convince him that we needed more money for the party's marketing programme and the conversation drifted around to the necessity for achieving consistency of the party's brand positioning.

At the time Nadir controlled the Del Monte processed fruit company, whose brand positioning was a reassurance of quality – the reassurance being provided in the advertising by the 'Man from Del Monte ('e say YES!!)' – a wondrously effective advertising property. Having heard that some new managers had arrived at the company I bet my lunch guest that sooner or later someone would suggest dropping 'the Man', because 'he is no longer relevant to today's consumer'. New brooms for some reason always use that daft expression. Nadir was politely sceptical that anyone could ever conceive of such a silly plan, but I was not particularly surprised to read a few months later that reports were circulating to just that effect. The new brooms had struck again, but luckily for the company, sanity was later restored and the Man from Del Monte was reinstated. Many brands do not escape this fate so easily, however.

This is not to say that times don't change and brand positionings sometimes have to change with them. Thirty years ago a young man called Brian Epstein took a greasy, leather-clad group of rock and roll delinquents just back from performing in Hamburg's red-light district and repositioned them as a cheerful, declassé, be-suited, non-smoking, non-drinking, non-womanizing group of young musicians loved by parents and teenagers alike. The result was a very profitable phenomenon called Beatlemania. Mick Jagger cleverly spotted the obvious alternative positioning that Epstein had left open. As Tom Wolfe once observed, 'The Beatles want to hold your hand, but the Stones want to burn your town.'

As young people's disposable income rose, an unsuccessful German-type clear beer was repositioned to be a youthful, sociable, fun drink – and lager louts were born. As these young Britons grew up, they took to the health and fitness craze in the 1980s, so SmithKline Beecham (as it is now) took their fizzy, glucose convalescent tonic, Lucozade, and repositioned it to become an 'energy-replacement' drink for the sports market – without changing a molecule of the product's formula.

As globalization took hold, British Airways repositioned themselves from being the patriotic choice ('Fly the Flag') to the best in the skies ('The World's Favourite Airline'). As competition from commercial broadcasting increased, the BBC repositioned itself away from 'Auntie' (Reithian, paternalistic and unsuccessfully chasing ratings) to the 'Beeb' (modern, efficient and with quality programmes).

Even nations themselves are subject to this process, although one can only regret that the English tourism marketing experts have chosen to replace faded Imperial glory with a historical theme-park called 'Ye Olde Englande' (the implication being that we have no future, just a profitable past).

## Brand Personality

Brands, like people, not only have values, they have – as David Ogilvy first pointed out – personalities too. Manufacturers tend to use design (packaging or corporate livery) to replace the role of clothes in expressing their difference from other brands, but the intent is identical. Service companies use their employees, like switchboard operators, receptionists, waiters, cabin crew and shop assistants, to achieve the same objective. They can be young and lively ('NatWest') or old and stately (Coutts & Co). They can be friendly (Singapore Airlines) or brisk (Lufthansa).

However, the revolution that Peters and Waterman's book (*In Search of Excellence*) started seems to have left the retail sector behind. The High Street shops' image often rests on the impression that is conveyed by groups of surly 'security guards' lounging about the entrance. The Victorian shopkeepers knew how to make a customer genuinely welcome, as is evidenced by those shops that have survived. When, at Huntsman, Mr Maynard escorts you to the door and civilly wishes you a good day, one is reminded that informed and courteous service is not yet dead.

In the travel sector, British Airways is rightly held up as a model of customer service, born out of their 'Putting People First' training programme, and Sir Colin Marshall's experience at Avis, owner of probably the most famous and effective customer service challenger positioning ever ('We try harder'). Avis was largely the creation of the legendary Robert Townsend who said 'The only image you should care about is the smile on the face of your customer as he enjoys your product or on the face of your stockholder as he scans the company profits.' The word stockholder was changed in later editions to 'employee'.

*The Disney image*

This reliance on 'employee impression' can sometimes be taken too far. The staff of the Euro Disney theme-park outside Paris are issued with a ten-page guide on personal grooming. In it, they are told that women may wear earrings (but only smaller than a penny in diameter), but beards and dyed hair (on either sex) are banned. Only one ring per hand may be worn, and both smoking and drinking are banned. A team of 'grooming officers' tour the park looking for transgressors. How Orwell would have smiled to read this.

## Choosing a leader's image

Leaders and their personalities are used in exactly the same way by political image makers. Everyone's physical appearance, background and character are complex enough to produce several different choices of image. Take John Major, for example. His negative attitude to image making, though misguided, is perfectly genuine. His chief press secretary confirmed to me that he 'had never discussed image making with the prime minister'. However, his image makers (should he ever choose to overturn his promise not to use them) could emphasize his comparative youth, good looks, energy, determination and love of sport; or they could choose to emphasize his modest social background, ordinary tastes, common touch, courtesy, calmness and modesty. The former (let's call it the J F Kennedy strategy) would be suitable if he was a visionary seeking radical change. The latter (the 'Lincoln') is suitable only if he wishes to preserve the status quo. But the truth is that both are equally valid, both being equally true descriptions of his personality.

The amount that the image makers have to rely on personality, rather than policy, obviously depends on how far apart the two contenders in an election are. When the two parties' ideological centres of gravity are converging rather than diverging, personality is likely to become a more important way for the voter to determine credibility. The Tory party will, therefore, no doubt claim to be competent, while also being caring. The Labour party will no doubt claim to be caring, while also being competent. The credibility of these claims will increasingly rest on the voter's perception of how the leaders' personalities substantiate the positionings.

## The image of the institutions

These positioning techniques are also extensively used by the institutions of both the power élite and the influence élite. The home civil service continues its worthy attempts to replace an élitist Oxbridge caste image with a meritocratic, professional one, although, apart from the 'Next Steps' programme, it is not achieving a great deal of success. The diplomatic service continues to entertain the taxpayer with stories of waste, extravagance, over-manning, incompetence and a promotion policy known as 'buggins turn' (*cf* the Plowden Report 1964; Duncan 1968, Berrill 1977 *ad nauseam*). Happily, the BBC's World Service continues to convey an image of a country whose values of honesty, fairness, accuracy and objectivity are still the norm. As for 'The Friends' (as SIS are called in Whitehall), after Burgess, Maclean, Philby, Blunt, Cairncross and heaven knows who else, Fleming and Le Carré have come to their rescue. I simply note the late Sir Maurice Oldfield's (formerly chief of MI6) opinion that 'military intelligence has the same kind of relationship to real intelligence, as military music has to real music'.

The armed forces have been possibly the most successful of the governing élites in repositioning themselves, moving from a low-tech, amateur, conscript organization to a professional group of highly skilled technicians. The SAS have taken over from the Guards as the army's crack regiment, by a mixture of clever image building based on mystique (often a very effective way of mythologizing an organization, eg Mossad and Opus Dei, not least because it hides their mistakes from our view, making them seem omnipotent and infallible) and restricted public exposure at places like Mogadishu and Princes Gate.

The armed services, the police and the Roman Catholic church have made extensive use of modern marketing techniques, especially advertising. In the case of the Roman Catholic church, the Vatican commissioned an advertising campaign in the early 1990s to solicit tax-deductible donations. The campaign logo was a basket containing loaves and fishes!

In the case of the police this has concentrated on replacing *Dixon of Dock Green* with a multicultural intake of better educated and better trained personnel. Recent developments range from the launch of a guide to plain English (to replace that curious officialese which made police constables stock figures of middle-class mockery), to proposals to recruit homosexuals of both sexes. A recent advertisement for the accelerated promotion scheme for graduates reinforced the police's emphasis on marketing. It was headlined 'You could go far in public relations' and used the fact that PR is an integral part of a senior police officer's job, to attract candidates.

## Advertising in the political process

When British journalists think of modern marketing techniques, like advertising, being used in politics, they generally think of the 1979 General Election. However, the election that really started this trend took place exactly 20 years earlier. As Butler and Rose noted at the time, the Tory party's campaign in that election year (and the two preceding years) was the first in Britain to follow America's lead and use techniques designed to ensure that 'favourable associations were conjured up by the mention of the party's name, rather than expounding policies'. They noted that this campaign was based on four basic principles: exposure to image making long before the election takes place; simple language and issues of everyday relevance; outside experts being indispensable; and the idea that image making is a complement to, but not a substitute for, policy.

Colman, Prentis and Varley (then one of Britain's leading advertising agencies) had been hired by the Tories in 1949 for a two-year period to carry out advertising prior to the 1951 General Election and were brought back in 1957 to prepare a press advertising campaign which started on 30 June when a Gallup poll put the Labour party 7 per cent ahead. The advertising CPV produced rehearsed themes that are still used today. 'The Conservatives are the Party of the Whole Country' (*cf* 'classlessness'), or 'Conservatives – working for a world of opportunity', or (in the election campaign itself) 'Life's better with the Conservatives. Don't let Labour ruin it.' (*cf* 1987:

'Britain is great again. Don't let Labour wreck it.').

## *Picture research*

Research was used for the first time in Britain to fine-tune the photographs they used. Pictures of primary-school-age children were replaced with ones showing teenagers in school uniforms, when researchers found the audience was mostly concerned with getting their older children places in grammar schools. These photographs were carefully chosen to appeal to the various target groups that had been isolated, ie housewives, prosperous C2s and young voters. The ads in the *News of the World* featured a cloth-capped skilled workman, in the *Sunday Pictorial* a modern working woman and in the *Observer* a scientist. As the economy boomed, the photographs changed to a family gathered around a table groaning with food and a TV set in the corner (70 per cent of homes now had one), and in another ad the family washed their new car outside their new house.

'Feel good' was the objective and, as the economy improved (unemployment fell by half a million, and GDP and real wages both rose leading to a credit boom), the Tory posters had the desired effect.

## *TV election broadcasts*

In the election campaign itself attention focused on the party election broadcasts, although here Labour heavily outgunned the Tories. Their *Britain Belongs to You* series (introduced by a young, ex-BBC producer MP called Anthony Wedgwood Benn, who subsequently became Viscount Stansgate. Also appearing was an ex-journalist MP called Woodrow Wyatt, who subsequently became Lord Wyatt of Weeford) was very good television (not surprisingly, as the format was modelled on the popular BBC *Tonight* magazine programme), while the first Tory effort of five cabinet ministers sitting around in Birch Grove was a dull throwback to another era. After much press criticism, Christopher Chataway was brought in to interview ministers and host the programme and, in the election eve broadcast, Norman Collins produced a 15-minute Macmillan solo effort to universal applause from the press.

## *The only point of an election campaign . . .*

The parallels with the 1987 General Election campaign are obvious. The issue of the *New Statesman* published before the 1959 results were known called Labour's campaign 'a signal and significant success'. In the same way, the media gave the 1987 campaign to Labour, Peter Mandelson (Director of Campaigns and Communications at Labour HQ) unwisely going as far as to boast later 'We won the campaign'. His verdict was obviously a foolish one, as the only point of any campaign is to win an election. Although I respected Mandelson's abilities as a news manager, comments like these made me realize that he was only a gifted amateur when it came to advertising, with the good sense to surround himself with first-division professionals.

Well, the Tories won that election (by 102 seats), as they had done in 1959 (by 101). Much more to the point, the Labour party in 1959 had seen that the marketing of politics was possible and, in a close election, it was easy to see that it could make the difference between winning and losing. Gaitskell led the move away from an ideologically biased attitude to image making, saying that the lesson of the election was that they 'must revise altogether our ideas of how much money we should be raising and spending for posters and other forms of propaganda'. Both parties had now accepted that the new techniques brought over from America were indispensable to the political process and both were equally set on using marketing to win the next election – whenever it should come.

## Attack campaigns

Both the 1964 elections had a common thread running through them: John Fitzgerald Kennedy. Harold Wilson had been impressed with the youthful energy and panache of Kennedy's first few months in office, promising a similar '100 days of dynamic action', and as a result he ran a virtually presidential campaign. Johnson draped Kennedy's civil rights mantle over himself and preached a crusade for a new New Deal called the 'Great Society'.

The summer of 1964 saw the fully-fledged arrival of a marketing phenomenon that still causes controversy today – the 'attack campaign'. 'Knocking copy' is an age-old technique in consumer marketing, but in modern times it has been tightly controlled by regulatory authorities. Negative political advertising has no such constraints and both 1964 elections saw a violent explosion of sophisticated abuse.

On 19 March 1964, Lyndon Johnson's representatives signed a contract with the advertising agency Doyle, Dane Bernbach to handle the Democratic presidential campaign. The agency was run by Bill Bernbach, who had revolutionized advertising in the late 1950s and early 1960s with outstandingly effective campaigns for the Volkswagen Beetle and Avis which had been noticed by Kennedy.

The agency pored over Johnson's opponent's speeches, which were a rich mine of Goldwater gaffes on nuclear weapons and social security. Despite polls showing Johnson leading Goldwater 62–29, the president was determined to crush him utterly and, believing DDB could be the hammer to do this, increased their advertising budget. DDB used this munificence in an all-out effort to scare America. Goldwater was painted as a trigger-happy extremist (using Goldwater's statement against him: 'Extremism in the defense of liberty is no vice. Moderation in the pursuit of justice is no virtue', which is a loose paraphrase of Cicero) who would send nuclear missiles to the Soviet Union on the slightest pretext; who would abolish social security and sell off the Tennessee Valley Authority; and who thought the country would be better off if the eastern seaboard were to be cut off from the rest of America and floated off into the Atlantic.

The ads that claimed Goldwater wanted to abolish social security were clever, memorable and palpably dishonest. Goldwater had been quite clear that he wished to make the system voluntary (and therefore solvent). In a striking parallel with the Labour party's recent 'the Tories are going to privatize the NHS' campaign, DDB's strategy was to throw muddy inferences at the Arizona Senator until some stuck.

The Democrats then attacked Goldwater by accusing him of not being a real Republican, giving permission to worried Republicans to abandon Goldwater on the grounds that he did not deserve any party loyalty. DDB scripted an ad called 'Confession of a Republican' where an actor, in an apparently unscripted fashion, meditates on why (despite his Republican loyalties) he is going to vote for Johnson, ending on the thought that, because the Ku Klux Klan were supporting Goldwater, he had definitely decided to vote against him.

It is difficult to believe that this farrago of lies, half-lies, half-truths, misquotations and downright smears could have got worse, but DDB had other ideas. It is no exaggeration to say that what the agency then went on to produce and air on 7 September 1964 was and is the most notorious example of attack advertising in modern political history.

## Dirty pictures

The ad opens with a pretty, blonde child standing in a grassy field. She is holding a daisy and picking the petals off one by one. As each petal falls she is heard counting from one to nine; on nine, a stern male voice takes over and reverses the sequence. As the camera zooms into the little girl's face we realize that the voice represents a missile launch countdown. At zero the screen explodes into the mushroom cloud of a nuclear blast. Johnson's voice is heard over this appalling image of violent death. 'These are the stakes. To make a world in which all of God's children can live, or go into the dark. We must either love each other or we must die.' The viewers' reaction was, of course, predictable: they interpreted the ad as meaning that the result of a vote for Goldwater was a vote for a nuclear holocaust, as they were indeed meant to.

The DDB copywriter who wrote the ads unashamedly admitted to basing the technique on Rorschach ink-blot psychiatric tests. The audience were left to see what he called 'the dirty pictures' in the images. Johnson's reaction was brief, scatological and swift. He ordered the ad off the air immediately. His action, however, was irrelevant. Such was the public and media reaction that the networks endlessly replayed the ad in their newscasts. The more the Republicans cried foul, the more the media ran the ad. The Democrats quickly released the news that the 'Daisy' ad would not run again. DDB had, however, prepared two more ads in the same vein.

In the first a young girl lovingly licks an ice-cream cone while the announcer implies that under President Goldwater it will be full of Strontium 90. In the second, a pregnant woman and her daughter stroll through a park while the announcer talks about the harm the unborn child could suffer from the fall-out produced by the Goldwater-inspired nuclear testing. The Democratic campaign team approved the first ad, but baulked at the second on the grounds that it was unsupported by any scientific evidence. Johnson's campaign slogan was 'The stakes are too high for you to stay at home', and the American people, now terrified of Goldwater, gave the president the enormous landslide victory he hungered for.

After the 'Daisy' broadcast, political advertising was never the same again. In the run-up to the 1970 election, the Labour party ran the notorious 'Yesterday's Men' advertising showing Heath, Home, Macleod and others in a lurid poster aimed at destroying their personal credibility and fitness to govern. In a very bad-tempered 1974 campaign *ad hominem* abuse of Wilson was commonplace in Tory broadcasts. By the end of the decade knocking copy had become part of the scene as a recital of the headlines produced by Saatchi & Saatchi in 1978 ('Educashun isn't working'; Britain isn't getting any better'; 'Labour isn't working'; and, best of all, 'Cheer up. They can't last for ever') and 1983 ('Like your manifesto, Comrade') shows. (The poster 'Labour isn't working' was said to have influenced Callaghan's decision not to call a General Election. In fact, Lord Callaghan confirmed in a letter to me that the poster campaign did not play any significant part in his decision. 'I saw no reason', he wrote, 'to hold an election at a time when it was not at all clear that we could win.')

### The Bush campaign

The debate concerning knocking copy erupted yet again in 1988, when the Bush campaign featured vintage examples of the genre, as ferociously effective as the 'Daisy' ad.

The Bush team consisted of three of the most experienced and successful image makers in politics. The campaign manager was Lee Atwater, the first political consultant to manage a presidential campaign. Atwater, a 37-year-old Georgian, first met Bush in 1973 when the latter was chairman of the Republican National Committee and Atwater was (at 21) working for the College Republican's national office. His main sources of ideas, he later said, came from Plato's *Republic*, Machiavelli's *The Prince* and Sun Tzu's *The Art of War*, and it showed. His personal motto was taken from his favourite Confederate general, Nathan Bedford Forrest: 'Get there firstest with the mostest.'

In 1980 Atwater was a consultant to southern Republican politicians and was soon at the centre of a 'dirty tricks' controversy. His client was a South Carolina congressman seeking to unseat a Democratic incumbent. At the opponent's press briefing, a reporter stood up and asked the congressman to comment on allegations that he had undergone psychiatric treatment and electro-shock therapy. Outraged by this, and suspecting an Atwater-inspired plot, the Democrats protested to Atwater. His reply (which has gone down in American political history as winning the 'throwing gasoline on the fire while pretending to put it out' award) was that he would not respond to someone who, in his words, 'had been hooked up to jumper cables'.

His reputation made, he became (at 33) director of the Reagan–Bush re-election campaign, steering the incumbents to an easy victory and, in 1988, Bush picked him yet again to manage the Republican campaign. In turn, Atwater selected the most successful political advertising consultant ever, Roger Ailes, known as 'The Old Fox'. Ailes had started out as a producer on the *Mike Douglas Show* and had attracted Nixon's interest when the candidate had appeared on the programme. Ailes produced Nixon's TV specials in 1968, featuring in the Joe McGinnis hatchet job *The Selling of the President* and in every important election race since then. The third man was Robert Teeter, who had replaced Dick Wirthlin as the Republicans' pollster.

The trio got to work first on Bush (slowing down his speech and training him to keep his eyes still when speaking) and then on his opponent – safe in the knowledge they had the vice-president's full backing. As Ailes said later, 'Bush is like a pit bull with no fear. Tell him where to go and who to bite – and he's on him.' Their candidate being 17 points behind, the team recommended an 'attack' strategy.

Using focus groups, they identified four basic areas for the advertising: 'Dukakonimics – deriding the governor's economic record in Massachusetts; crime – especially the policy of prison furloughs; his lack of foreign policy experience; and his membership of the 'pointy-headed Liberal' club. 'The Fox' went to work and produced a three-pronged campaign. First, Dukakis was attacked as unpatriotic, the evidence being that he had vetoed legislation requiring teachers to lead their classes in the pledge of allegiance. Secondly, they undermined his managerial competence and environmentalist credentials by showing how Boston harbour had become a byword for pollution under the Dukakis administration.

Lastly and most importantly, they unleashed their secret weapon – Willie Horton. Horton had been convicted of murder and, while out on furlough from a Massachusetts prison, had been arrested for rape and the torture of the victim's boyfriend. 'If I can make Willie Horton a household name,' Atwater said, 'we'll win the election.' The Ailes team turned the Horton story into a grim, grainy, black-and-white film of a line of convicts going, not through the prison gate to pay the price of their terrible crimes, but instead into a revolving 'furlough' door, where they promptly re-emerged back out on the streets for an immediate resumption of their long careers as serial murderers. The Dukakis lead simply vanished, evaporated by the heat of the Republican advertising. James Baker (the Bush campaign chairman) mixed this attack campaign with 'kinder, gentler' Bush imagery based on social and environmental caring. By the time the election came, Bush was so far in front, that Dukakis was beaten before the polls opened.

Atwater had proved exactly what he had set out to prove, that negative advertising works and, in the process, transformed George Bush into a winner. Two years later, suffering from inoperable brain cancer, Atwater defended the campaign, but not his own role in it. As he was dying, he wrote that he was sorry that he had said of Dukakis that he 'would strip the back off the little bastard ... and make Willie Horton his running mate'. When finally he died on 29 March 1991, the obituaries recorded not this death-bed regret but the authentic Atwater: 'My job is the politics of politics. The contest, the winning and losing is big for me. I can't stand to lose.'

### Negative advertising by other means

Atwater was essentially right. Negative advertising does work.

Indeed, it works so effectively that the UK Takeover Panel has now has banned the use of it in contested bids. (See Rule 90 of the Takeover Panel's Code.) There are also very strict restrictions on knocking copy in commercial advertising.

When I put this point to Barry Delaney (one of the Labour party's principal advertising consultants) he agreed. 'In recent years in this country', he says, 'all the most memorable ads are Tory party knocking ads and the value of them is that they encourage your own supporters, discourage waverers and infuriate and demoralize the opposition.'

'Although the extent of their contribution cannot be researched,' he says, 'because people won't admit they are influenced by advertising, knocking copy, when it's well done, is probably going to be more effective than any other kind of advertisement.'

John Salmon (the creator of some of the best Tory PPBs of recent years) warns, however, that there is a line you must not cross. 'If you run an ad saying Kinnock is a Welsh half-wit and show him falling into the sea, it would surely backfire.' He makes the point that your own side would probably feel very uncomfortable with this approach and it would also only stiffen the sinews of Kinnock's supporters, encouraging them on to greater efforts.

Peter Gummer (who is one of John Major's principal communications advisers) maintains that the most effective advertising is a well-aimed, policy-based attack on the opposition, using the right tone of voice, one that matches the party's (and leader's) personality.

Over the last decade in Britain the pros and cons of attack advertising, using the person rather than the policy, have been largely irrelevant as the political leaders have not allowed such attacks. Margaret Thatcher was certainly very strict on this issue and refused utterly to countenance any attacks on Neil Kinnock, other than an ability to do the job of prime minister that he was applying for. True, Kinnock approved Labour's notorious 'Gilbert and Sullivan' party election broadcast in 1987, but it was so painfully amateurish and obviously offensive that it can only have served to gain sympathy for the prime minister.

Not that exactly the same effect can't be achieved by other means. For instance, when Carter opposed Edward Kennedy in the 1980 primaries, he was advised to contrast his stable family life with Kennedy's broken marriage and troubled private life. Carter's advertising team came up with the 'non-attack' attack formula of showing the president helping his daughter Amy with her homework while the voice-over intoned, 'Husband. Father. President. He's done these three jobs with distinction.'

Another way of achieving the same end was also used by Reagan in 1980. The anti-Carter ads that year were all produced by independent 'political action committees' so that Reagan was not tarred with the knocking brush. This technique has also been used in Britain, most recently both by Aims of Industry and the rogue organization formed by the right winger David Hart to oppose trade union power in the 1987 election.

## Why does advertising work?

Political advertising works (whether it is positive or negative) only by chiming in with what the voter already thinks, therefore reinforcing their beliefs. It provides a focus of other campaigning activities and helps set an agenda. Campaigns have to be balanced, because an uninterrupted diet of negative advertising would be unacceptable to party and media, while a completely positive campaign simply wouldn't be effective. A good example of this proposition was the 1989 Euro-election, when a series of 'pro-Europe' ads that Tim Bell prepared for the Tory party (eg one said 'Britain our home. Europe our future') were unfortunately turned down by No 10 and (ignorant of this fact) the media attacked the campaign as too negative.

Norman Tebbit aimed for a 60:40 positive:negative ratio in the 1987 General Election and that seems about right.

Sometimes just the fact of advertising is enough. In 1989 the British Medical Association ran an extensive advertising campaign against the government's health reforms. Although the ads themselves weren't very effective in their arguments, their tone of voice ('hopping mad' would be a reasonable summary) was. They alerted the public to the doctors' strength of feeling on the issue and attracted a large amount of support from a previously unconcerned citizenry on the simple grounds that, if the doctors were against self-governing hospitals or GP budgets, then so were they.

To those who think that advertising has magical and devilish powers of persuasion, let me say this: advertising, like fashion, mostly works at the level (to take an example from Roland Barthes) of a wrestling match, where the spectators know perfectly well that neither wrestler is genuinely hurting the other. The audience merely appreciates the style, expertise and wit that goes into the performance. They are not taken in by falsity. The conspiracy theorists overestimate the advertisers' talent and underestimate the audience's commonsense, seeing them as gullible, inadequate or naïve. As David Ogilvy warned his fellow advertising executives (in a more unconsciously sexist time), 'The consumer is not a moron, she's your wife'. The fact is that advertising experts are flattered by attacks on them by the Vance Packards and the JK Galbraiths of this world. Packard's book *The Hidden Persuaders* and Galbraith's *The Affluent Society* both sought to represent advertising as a social evil. It makes them feel important (they aren't) and powerful (ditto).

To those who think advertising can sell someone something they don't either need or want, let me say only two words: Ford Edsel. Still not convinced? OK, how about 'New Coke'?

*The clues*

The truth is that no one knows how advertising works, just that some of it does. We do, however, have some clues. There does not seem to be any exact relationship between recall of a campaign and better sales, but I would find it difficult to argue that *not* being able to remember the brand's advertising is a good thing. Similarly, it seems reasonable to suppose that liking or respecting the brand is not entirely a bad idea.

It bothers the advertising fraternity that they are not mechanics of the psyche, technicians who have a complete explanation for all the intricate wiring in the human brain that is involved in interpreting communications from the outside. They would much prefer it if they could come up with an all-embracing theory to explain how advertising works and so, every once in a while, someone arrives with another new thesis which becomes fashionable (until replaced by yet another). In fact, no notice should be taken of any of them. All anyone need remember is that advertisements should make the audience remember the brand and its benefit. It's as simple as that.

As to advertising's effectiveness in the political process, more rain forests have disappeared in the cause of truth on this subject than on any other – all to no avail. These endless, pseudo-scientific studies purporting to audit the effects of political advertising campaigns are a pointless waste of time, because even if anyone did believe the result, what could they do with the information? If, as some academics maintain, advertising can make a difference of up to 2 per cent, what action could the parties take on this basis? What academics mostly don't realize is that politics is like the high jump, where you use *all* the assets at your disposal to clear the bar. You never risk the disqualification that comes from knocking it off, so you always spend as much as you can afford and try your damndest to make an impact.

If, as in 1983, it is obvious that the opposition is well and truly beaten, then cancelling £3 million of the £10 million advertising budget (as Cecil Parkinson did) is perfectly sensible, but in any other circumstance it is far too risky. Rich and in opposition is not an enviable position to find oneself in. On a trans-Atlantic flight someone once asked the chewing gum tycoon, Philip K Wrigley, why he continued to spend so much money on advertising when his business was already such a success. 'For the same reason', replied Wrigley, 'that the pilot of this plane keeps the engine running when we're already 30,000 ft up in the air.'

## Marketing the personality

### *The packaging of Ted Heath*

By the late 1960s the image makers had taken over the asylum. In 1968 they were given their first opportunity to capture a senior British politician and practise their arts uninterrupted. The story of their failure is both an interesting and instructive one. When Geoffrey Tucker took over at Central Office as director of publicity (on secondment from Young & Rubicam), his principal was seen as unpopular, aloof, cold and incapable of projecting any kind of favourable image on television.

Tucker had a simple strategy. 'I wanted the viewers to think of him', he said, 'as Ted Heath rather than Mr Edward Heath.' He gathered together an extraordinary array of top image makers:

James Garrett (commercials producer); Ronnie Millar (play-wright and speechwriter); Barry Day (copywriter); Terry Donovan (photographer and director); Bryan Forbes (film director); and Gordon Reece (TV director), who were called the 'Thursday Team'.

This group has every claim to be the most talented gathering of communications advisers ever recruited for a political campaign anywhere, easily outclassing the 1987 Labour team. They immediately set about coaching Heath on his television appearances. Heath, in private, had a pleasant conversational voice, yet in public spoke in a pompous, long-winded way. The Team arranged for secret video-recording sessions with their principal to try and get him to reproduce on camera the attractive way of speaking he had in private – in other words, to be himself. Tucker provided the questions, Donovan played the aggressive interviewer, and Day then analyzed Heath's performance.

Only a minor improvement was noted by the media, but the Team persevered in their strategy of making Heath approach-able. This time Forbes followed him around with a hand-held camera on a north-east tour. Heath was shown talking to the people in a friendly and down-to-earth way. Tucker started to fill in other areas of Heath's personality and was particularly successful in getting coverage for his hobby of sailing. A TV special, *Sportsnight with Coleman*, followed. Tucker then arranged for the shadow cabinet's election planning meeting at Selsdon Park in Croydon to be given the full treatment (depressing and infuriating Wilson).

To overcome his remote, bachelor image the team then invited the media to film Heath and a young woman going sailing together, but Heath (who had never met the woman before) ruined the photo-opportunity by telling reporters that she was 'only the cook'. The Team then decided that they would copy the Labour party's new-fangled 'walkabouts', but Heath invariably spoilt these by his acting (in Michael Cockerell's description) 'in the manner of an orderly officer asking his men if there were any complaints'.

The press were unanimous. Wilson's campaign was 'brilliant' and Heath had already lost. The bookmakers refused all further bets when Labour reached 33–1 on to win. In fact, all Tucker's team's hard work to humanize Heath was largely a waste of time. Where they truly did make a difference was in convincing the voters that Wilson was not to be trusted with Britain's economic future. Yet again, a good challenger strategy had beaten a weak brand leader strategy. The Thursday Team celebrated at Chequers that Sunday, but no more attempts were made to turn Mr Heath into 'Ted'.

## Kinnock – the movie

In 1987, the Labour party's equivalent to the Thursday Group, the Shadow Communications Agency (SCA), tried again to market a leader's personality, with different methods, but with the same result. From 1979 to 1985 the Labour party's reputation with the electorate was at an all-time low. Increasingly, they were seen to have abandoned the idea that working people should be helped upwards and replaced it with the idea that the fortunate or enterprizing should be levelled down. The result was that neither group looked forward to their fate. Crosland's view of socialism as inherently expressing an enjoyment of life was choked by a fog of egalitarianism, puritanism and punitive taxation. An insistent anti-business stance was expressed by both the Labour party establishment and the annual conference, and this also pervaded their view of party marketing.

Neil Kinnock's election as party leader in 1983 changed all that. By 1987 a team of marketing professionals had been put together under the chairmanship of Peter Mandelson and it was this team that produced *Kinnock – the Movie*. The chief talent among Labour's Shadow Communications Agency was Chris Powell, a shrewd and experienced strategist from BMP. His brother (now Sir) Charles Powell, Mrs Thatcher's foreign affairs private secretary, was the most influential official in No 10 and (due to his extensive press contacts) an important image maker.

The motivation for the broadcast was simple and followed the same basic reasoning that inspired the Heath re-packaging. Patricia Hewitt, Kinnock's press secretary, felt very strongly that the public saw Kinnock through the distorting mirror of the 'Tory' press and if only they knew the real Kinnock.... In fact, as one of Kinnock's close associates told me, Kinnock's poor relations with the press were largely his own fault. He increasingly disliked and distrusted the lobby, and became less and less concerned with what the journalists felt or said about him. What the Tories had taught him, however, was first, that good communications with the voters were essential and second, these could only be created with outside help. The SCA were also greatly helped in this by the 'success' of the GLC's advertising campaign. It didn't work, but some in the media were naïvely impressed by its professionalism and the Labour Left's anti-advertising bias was subsequently toned down.

The logo change (which contrary to reports was Kinnock's own idea) and the 1986 'Freedom and Fairness' campaign were a success in that they convinced the press that the party wanted to change and therefore perhaps wanted government. The *Financial Times* of 23 April went as far as saying 'The British Labour Party is again beginning to look like a credible party of government'. The press, however, still hadn't changed its attitude to Kinnock.

Hugh Hudson (like Bryan Forbes before him) had volunteered his services to direct the film. But the actual format was secretly devised by executives from Doak & Schrum, the Virginia-based firm of political consultants, flown in especially for that purpose. As the company was well known for its attack campaigns (later most notably in the Richards-Mattox Texas gubernatorial race in 1991), knowledge of their input into the Labour party's plans (which goes on to this day) was kept highly confidential, even from senior shadow cabinet members. The Doak & Schrum personnel were brought specially to London in order to outline to the Labour team how successful 'bio-pic' formats had been put together for US candidates, eg the Reagan film, *This is a Man*. The idea was to get Kinnock to be himself, so Hudson searched for an interviewer who could draw him out. It was an inspired choice to pick Alastair Campbell, who was then the *Daily Mirror's* political editor and a close friend of the Kinnocks. This footage, shot in the sitting room of the Kinnock's Ealing home, was very effective at showing the Labour leader *au naturel*. Gone was the mistrustful stare and defensive body language; this was more like two friends having a relaxed chat.

Hudson then took from 'library' film Kinnock's speech from the 1985 party conference, when he verbally thrashed the Militant council in Liverpool, while one of its principal officers,

Derek Hatton, shouted 'Liar!' at him from the floor (this had been secretly researched using the US people meter technique). This was intercut with some unsuccessful testimonials from James Callaghan and Barbara Castle and some dramatic footage of Mr and Mrs Kinnock walking on some cliffs near Llandudno. Hudson's filming was in the Reagan style laid down by Doak & Schrum (although the British press were not to know this), and his post-production, ie editing, music (by Michael Kamen), dubbing etc was first class.

The broadcast was aired on 21 May and the media reaction was uniformly favourable. The *Sunday Times* called it 'masterly' and said it 'broke new ground in TV political history'. Foolishly, the Tories complained of 'glossy packaging', which got the film even more coverage, so much so that Labour decided to run it again – although, because of complaints from inside the party about a 'cult of personality', the end frame of 'Kinnock' was changed to 'Labour' and a brief clip of the shadow cabinet was added. In fact, this decision to re-broadcast was especially foolish as it meant Labour had to abandon a broadcast on the health service which could actually have won them some votes.

What happened next is familiar to hundreds of marketing managers, who have been sold a pup by advertising agencies out to make an 'art' film about a poor product. It had no effect whatsoever – at least, not on the only target group that really matters – floating voters.

The Labour hype machine, however, went into overdrive. So effective was this operation that one still reads to this day fantastical accounts of Kinnock's rating 'rising by 16 points' in a matter of days. The *Sunday Times*/MORI table below tells the true story.

*Q:* Who do you think would make the most capable prime minister?

|  | Week 1 | Week 2 | Week 3 | Week 4 |
|---|---|---|---|---|
| Mrs Thatcher | 46% | 46% | 45% | 45% |
| Mr Kinnock | 21% | 24% | 26% | 27% |
| Dr Owen | 13% | 12% | 13% | 13% |
| Mr Steel | 10% | 9% | 9% | 8% |
| No opinion | 10% | 9% | 7% | 7% |

What happened was that Kinnock's rating among those *already intending to vote Labour* rose from an embarrassing 66 per cent to a semi-respectable 82 per cent. In the heat of the election, Labour's claims that the broadcast had created a potential prime minister out of Mr Kinnock were taken by harassed journalists at face value. Before long the myth was firmly established: even some Tories believed it. The banal truth was that people liked the film and its professionalism, but they had no intention of voting for Labour simply because Mr Kinnock was perhaps a nicer man than they had previously given him credit for. Labour's claim that it was 'the most effective piece of political communication in recent political history' was silly and naïve, especially as it was Kinnock himself who was about to help the Tories to create the most effective piece of political communication in the 1987 election.

## 'Labour's Policy on Arms'

On Sunday, 24 May, 18 days before polling day, Neil Kinnock appeared on TV-AM, interviewed by David Frost. Frost questioned Kinnock closely on how a country that had unilaterally disposed of its nuclear deterrent would oppose an invasion by a foreign power. Kinnock suggested that a government would use 'all the resources you have, to make any occupation totally untenable', and cited the Afghanistan Mujahadin guerillas as an example. The popular press knocked this novel policy, NATO's supreme commander denied reports that he had advocated the withdrawal of US troops if Labour won and President Reagan intervened to say that a unilateral Labour government would have to be persuaded that such a policy was 'a grievous error'.

Saatchi immediately capitalized on this error by producing an ad showing a British soldier with his hands held high in surrender, with the memorable and witty headline 'Labour's Policy on Arms'. Not only had Kinnock been shown to be advocating a very silly policy, but also that he did so while not being clever enough to avoid Frost's trap. I have no doubt that, along with effective attacks on Labour's economic incompetence, this ad gained more votes from floating voters than any other in the election campaign.

### And the moral is...

The moral of these two stories comes in six parts. First, no amount of talent or hype can convince the voter that a sow's ear is anything other than a part of the body female pigs use for hearing the swill-bucket's rattle.

Second, as ours is *not* a presidential system, parties matter more than leaders (no matter how much the media talk of personalities).

Third, a popular and respected leader in charge of an unpopular party will usually lose.

Fourth, an unpopular leader in charge of a popular party will probably win.

Fifth, no political image maker can afford to ignore the leader's personality or do anything other than try mightily to improve his or her image, but if this is at the expense of communicating the benefits of policy, then it's *always* the wrong strategic direction to choose.

Last, those who mistake what are called 'production values' (music, lighting, casting, editing etc) for content, are destined for a shock at the polls. Voters make a choice based on the credibility of promises, not on the track record of film directors. The medium in this instance is very definitely *not* the message.

## Direct marketing

While advertising's contribution to the political process has been vastly exaggerated by the party professionals' hype (which in turn has been swallowed by a largely naïve and ignorant media), the image makers have been careful to keep the real secret marketing weapon in the background. Direct marketing is defined by one of the world's leading experts, Drayton Bird, as 'any advertising activity which creates and exploits a direct relationship between you and your prospect (or customer) as an individual'. Indeed, in the business world, in a 1987 poll of the 250 top UK advertisers, 60 per cent thought that direct marketing would be *more* important than advertising to their business by the year 2000.

Direct marketing became important in politics for the same reason it became important in retailing, ie voters (like shoppers) are divided up into discrete geographically based units. They can be individually identified by name, gender and address; in fact, by 300 census variables. Database companies like CCN use their computers to calculate from the address the socio-economic group to which the inhabitants of the house belong.

In 1982, direct mail was introduced into the UK political process by the Tory party's director of marketing, Sir Christopher Lawson, not because of his experience as a senior executive of Mars, as some have said, but because he had, while employed by Mars in America, worked on various Republican congressional campaigns as a volunteer.

Lawson first tested direct mail in the tactical seats, both as part of a fund-raising campaign and to assess its ability to communicate the benefits of policy. The targets for the persuasional mailing were young householders and the results showed that it could be making as much as 3 per cent difference to the vote, which in these marginal seats (all of which the Tories won) was beyond price.

In the 1980s the parties tended to concentrate on fund-raising activities (especially the SDP, which collected 70 per cent of its 1987 election budget from direct mail), but quickly realized that persuasional direct marketing's impact on voters' attitudes in by-elections could be crucial. The example of the Australian Labour party, who retained power by a sophisticated programme of marketing, and the still highly classified results of an Israeli campaign, acted as an encouragement to all the parties. In Australia, Hawke's party professionals concentrated on the undecideds in marginal seats using the novel approach of sending out a questionnaire. The voters were asked for some basic information about themselves and, most importantly, to explain what issues they felt were the most significant to their lives. The computers then processed the answers and dispatched personal letters, addressed by name to the individual, explaining Labour party policy on the relevant issue and asking for a response. If the response was positive they continued to receive a flow of reassuring letters on the other issues that concerned them. If not, then further arguments were advanced and, if necessary, a party worker would be dispatched to preach the gospel.

Drayton Bird, who studied this outstandingly successful campaign carefully, wrote afterwards, 'Direct mail, with its ability to develop arguments and cover issues in detail, was the perfect medium and the sophisticated use of data enabled Labour to target the right promises to the right people.'

Now we have the required level of computer sophistication to process vast databases, direct mail and telephone 'selling' have the ability to make the difference between winning and losing. This, and not advertising, is the future of marketing, both in business and politics. Unfortunately, many politicians and their advisers don't have much (or even any) business experience to guide them and still fall easy prey to advertising agencies – who usually have no interest in pushing any marketing technique other than advertising.

## Conferences and rallies

Direct mail had been used extensively by religious organizations before British political parties grasped its true importance. Foremost among these was the Billy Graham organization, who had a computerized mailing list of 11 million people as early as 1963. Working for Graham at this time was a young man called Harvey Thomas and it was Thomas who introduced (or should I say re-introduced, as Goebbels had perfected controlled mass meetings 40 years previously) another new technique to politics: the use of stage-managed conferences and rallies to create an image for a political party. There had been rallies from time immemorial and annual conferences since 1868 but, other than US nominating conventions, little effort had gone into their presentation nor, until television, had there been any special need to.

Thomas had worked for Graham for 15 years, in 97 countries, producing his rallies or 'crusades' and had become expert at the stage-management of mass meetings. In 1978 he volunteered his part-time services as a consultant to Conservative Central Office to work on the planning for the General Election. While Geoffrey Tucker had arranged for travelling backdrops for Heath in 1970, the arts of presentation – eg advance planning, sets, lighting, camera angles, sound etc – had not been applied to

mass meetings covered by the media and, indeed, Thomas met
great resistance to change from the party organizers.

### In the mood

Thomas brought two simple principles to bear on the task.
'First', he says 'make it easy for the presenter to present, and
secondly, make it easy for the recipient to receive.' In line with
the latter, the entrances to the conference halls are now carefully
conceived to put the audience in a receptive mood and make
them feel comfortable and welcome in what to them is a strange
and perhaps unsettling environment. This 'user-friendly'
environment can be achieved not just by good signage, so that
the audience knows exactly where to go, but also by the warmth
of the stewards' welcome. (A lot of these techniques were
developed in the US service industry, eg the design of hotels,
restaurants and aeroplanes.)

As they enter the hall, the stage set is designed to produce the
right reaction of excited anticipation and deliver the communication strategy's objectives by means of a suitable slogan.
Although for some reason that is not clear, the media get very
excited about set designs, in fact the only point about them worth
noting is that, while a good set can't make a good speech, an
untidy, grubby or confusing set can ruin a good speech by
distracting the audience.

To make it easy for the speaker and to give them greater
authority, autocues were introduced from the US (where they
had first been used by the Democrats in 1964), together with
electronically controlled lecterns. These autocues work by
reflected light from concealed television screens, so the conference hall lighting has to be adjusted in order that it doesn't
'wipe' the two screens. Large television 'walls' are used to interest
the audience until the conference proper starts. The pictures
come from special closed-circuit cameras controlled by party
technicians.

At the start of an important event like a prime minister's
speech the right mood is induced by an initial release of tension.
This is done by carefully selected music which increases the
audience's involvement, by encouraging clapping and singing
along. Fifteen minutes before the speaker begins the tunes are

those which produce an involuntary response (hymns in the case of Graham, '*I Do Like to Be Beside the Seaside*' for party conferences) and the technicians turn the closed-circuit cameras on to the audience. An inevitable competition to get on the screen ensues and any lingering inhibitions start to fade away. The pace and the volume of the music is then increased imperceptibly. Banners, which have been distributed previously by party aides, are waved furiously. With only minutes to go before the speaker appears, a crescendo of music is produced and at the finish the screens show the source of the music (eg organist or band), and the audience applauds and settles back in anticipation. At this moment the platform party enters to the now inevitable applause; 'The audience', as Thomas puts it, 'now knows what is expected of them'.

Two minutes of silence then ensue, which increases the anticipation and revives the tension a little. It is at this point that the BBC floor manager takes control. The moment he receives the signal that the conference is being transmitted live, the prime minister walks on to the set and the audience bursts out into a roar of applause.

Inevitably, all of this has attracted comments about audience 'manipulation' and dark mutterings about Nuremberg. Obviously, any marketing technique can be used for evil just as easily as it can be used for good, but the premiss that audiences can be virtually hypnotized into doing something they don't want to do is quite clearly both wrong, and a belittlement of people's individualism. In fact the techniques used are simply those of the musical theatre and any large sporting occasion like the FA Cup final.

The use of outside conference design specialists to build sets; the use of lighting and music; the electronics of amplification; and the complex calculations needed to place television cameras for the best presentation of the speaker, were quickly taken up by the other parties and, in Labour's case, were again used as evidence by the media that the party was becoming more professional as its desire for power grew.

## Design

Another marketing technique was pressed into service in the

1980s, becoming more and more prominent in the process of gaining power – the use of design. I have explained (in Chapter 1) how Hitler and Mussolini had carefully chosen the symbols of their movements to express antecedents, and how Henry VII used the Tudor Rose to implement his strategy of legitimization. Similarly, the Confederacy had attempted to legitimize their secession from the Union by developing the 'stars and bars' battle flag.

The use of architectural design predated this activity by a long way. When Hammurabi built Babylon or Pericles the Parthenon, they were expressing their power through awe-inspiring arrangements in stone. In modern politics, the Capitol and the Houses of Parliament fulfil the same function. In business, the Edwardian banks used their opulent parlours to terrorize and cow their customers, while big business ambitions were efficiently expressed in the Flatiron, the Chrysler and the Sears skyscrapers, as the Egyptian pyramids and Bologna watchtowers had done before them. In doing so they have often reduced humans to insignificance, a trend that is hopefully being reversed due to the efforts of critics like the Prince of Wales. Although I am confident that Prince Charles did not do it for this reason, I cannot conceive of a better way of attracting the unanimous approbation of his future subjects than his heartfelt critique of architects (short, that is, of appearing at the windows of Kensington Palace urging the people to shoot all the town planners).

## Corporate identity programmes

As early as 1907, AEG were not only employing Behrens, the foremost designer of his age, but also Mies van der Rohe and Gropius.

The design explosion in the 1960s that produced everything from Vidal Sassoon's geometric cuts and Mary Quant cosmetics to Biba clothes and Habitat sofas, was driven by the new design consultancies like Pentagram and individuals like Michael Peters. What Alfred P Sloan, the chairman of General Motors, had discovered in the 1920s (ie *how* the car looked affected sales, just as much as how well it worked), was applied to the most mundane of objects. People not only became advertising literate owing to the efforts of the post-Bernbach style, but they were becoming 'style conscious' too.

## Political designs

At first, business embraced these new ideas more enthusiastically than political parties, but when Sir Christopher Lawson arrived from the former to advise the latter in 1981, the design revolution finally conquered the political process. Lawson was aghast to find that the Tory party effectively had no logo, just a collection of miscellaneous symbols representing each small outpost of it. He immediately set about remedying the situation, developing a design based on a combination of the Olympic flame and the Union Flag, which, after much opposition from the more old-fashioned wing of the party, was adopted for the 1983 election.

Following this lead, one of Neil Kinnock's first acts on becoming leader was to order that the old Labour party logo of a red flag be replaced by the socialist international symbol of a red rose. This version was subsequently redesigned (to remove a proletarian fist grasping the stem) and then featured extensively in literature and election advertising.

To the embarrassed horror of many MPs (and the cynical amusement of others), the Labour leadership were persuaded to speak on platforms behind vases of roses and to wear one in their buttonhole. It is a mark of Mr Kinnock's generosity of spirit that he allowed another to take the credit for his initiative.

In 1986 Jacques Delors hijacked the Council of Europe's flag with its 12 yellow stars in a circle on a blue background and began using it as the official flag of the EC (much to the impotent rage of the Council).

Neither Kenneth Baker nor I were happy with the Lawson logo when we arrived at party HQ in 1989, as it had by that time dated badly. We knew that if we replaced it with a new symbol (an oak tree was suggested), the media would assuredly interpret this as a move away from Thatcherism. I turned for help to Fiona Gilmore, a very talented design consultant from Michael Peters & Partners, and commissioned some qualitative research to see if the party chairman and I were right in our view that we could do better. Sure enough, we found out that few people could recognize the symbol (most could remember Labour's) and, when they were shown it, they thought it looked like a cross between an ice-cream cone and a Bulgarian conductor's cap badge. Worse than this, they thought it looked old-fashioned and dull, which, for a leadership committed to dynamic and radical change, was nothing less than a disaster. We decided to keep the Britishness of the red, white and blue colours, but to try and see if we could make the symbol more dynamic. Above all, we needed people to understand that it was a torch – in fact the torch of freedom.

So often, logos lose all meaning for the public because of the fashion for stylizing them out of all recognition. Companies like Shell, Lloyds Bank and Coca Cola, who really understand design, have over the years effectively modernized their symbols and I felt that this was the right evolutionary model for the party. The examples of others, like National Westminster Bank, British Telecom and Prudential served as a warning of what could happen if the 'new broom' mentality was allowed to take hold. Try this simple test for yourself. Take a sheet of paper, a pencil, and a) try and draw these three symbols from memory, then b) write down a convincing explanation of what they mean. Difficult, isn't it?

Fiona Gilmore and her team worked in the usual conditions of paranoid secrecy to produce a design which researched extremely well, people easily recognizing the torch form and (because of the association with the Statue of Liberty) correctly interpreting it as a symbol of the Tory party's guiding principle of individual freedom. I showed it to the prime minister, who was equally enthusiastic, and Kenneth Baker unveiled it at a special news conference on 25 September at the QEII Conference Centre just before the Blackpool conference. In only a matter of hours the media had taken it up, but without anyone interpreting it as a change of policy direction. Television constantly featured it as a simple, convenient graphic and the cartoonists had days of fun – all of which made the electorate aware of it very quickly – without the usual expensive awareness campaigns that business normally has to mount.

While one shouldn't overestimate the power of design, the right idea will work in a subtle and subliminal way that has important ramifications regarding an organisation's image. If you get it right, ie design a symbol that expresses the brand's *raison d'être* or its prime benefit, then you have established the foundations of a very strong positioning.

## Brand associations

Marketing has also brought to politics the practice of 'brand associations', with interesting if not entirely successful results. By associating one brand with another, some of the values of the more popular rub off on the less popular, ie acts as a testimonial for the other. Line extensions, as we have seen, borrow from the parent brand and the image of subsidiaries can be improved by reference to the parent group. This same mechanism can work by associating one group of people or an individual with another.

In the beginning, this idea was used mainly in the form of simple testimonials to the safety of new technology. For example, the Great Western Railway persuaded Prince Albert (who persuaded Queen Victoria) to endorse the new-fangled railway. The GWR built a station at Slough, near to Windsor Castle, and a special royal train. On 13 June 1842, with Isambard Kingdom Brunel himself on the footplate, the latest GWR locomotive *Phelegethon* conveyed Queen Victoria to Paddington in 30 minutes. The GWR were ecstatic at the public's quick response to Victoria's enthusiasm and the 1840s railway boom was on.

In a similar exercise, when the first escalator was installed at Earls Court underground station in 1911, a one-legged gentleman called 'Bumper' Harris was employed to stomp up and down the stairs on his peg leg to demonstrate the safety of the new device.

### *Personal endorsements*

The advertising world adopted the technique at a very early stage in the 20th century, using society matrons, sports personalities and Hollywood stars to endorse products. When it was discovered that the endorsement of the first of these categories was not working, they switched to using their domestic servants.

Since then dentists have recommended a toothpaste, a former Metropolitan Police commissioner has recommended a brand of tyre, breeders of pedigree dogs have endorsed a pet food, sporting heroes have put their faith in a hair cream, and so on. Even theft is another type of (unpleasant but) effective testimonial. The favourite target of today's 'ram raiders' is the Berghaus range of ski sportswear, while 'truck and winch' thieves select Harley-Davidson motorcycles for their export sales department.

## Showbiz endorsements

Politicians were quick to spot the power of this technique and they had a ready source of testimonial evidence from a group even more famous than them – movie stars. Orson Welles campaigned for Roosevelt, while Kennedy was surrounded by athletes, astronauts and, for the first time, black role models such as Harry Belafonte, Nat 'King' Cole and Lena Horne. Nixon had Sammy Davis Jnr in his corner, while Henry Fonda and Mary Tyler Moore endorsed Carter.

Pierre Salinger, in his memoirs, tells of a more practical use of actors when, in 1964, he went to campaign on his own behalf in Orange County, California, a stronghold of the far right-wing John Birch Society. Eggs and tomatoes rained down on his campaign train. In vain did Dick van Dyke and Angie Dickinson attempt to calm the crowd's fury. When, however, the massive bulk of Dan Blocker ('Hoss' in *Bonanza*) rose to speak there was, Salinger reports, a sudden and respectful silence.

Since 1979 all the main parties in Britain have assiduously courted show-business personalities for various lightweight roles at rallies and meetings. However, none of these have been used for any serious high-profile campaigning, as has been done in the States – perhaps because the UK does not have the kind of superstars the US does, or the same kind of star-struck attitudes that their population has.

The endorsement by Sean Connery of the Scottish Nationalists is an interesting development, but in my view this use of celebrities is unlikely to have the same level of effectiveness here as it does in the US. Certainly a large quantity of personalities endorsing a party may well convey an image of popularity, but British voters are too sensible to take the recommendations of actors, comedians and pop singers on Britain's future very seriously. The most effective use of celebrities is probably the endorsements of sportsmen and women to first-time voters.

### Product placement

In business, sponsorship of sporting occasions; television programmes; even 'quality of life' organizations like the National Trust (by British Gas), as well as the use of famous non-executive directors, play a similar role in increasing the prestige of large companies.

The most interesting marketing development, however, is in the growth of 'product placement', which is a particularly powerful brand association device. In many movies the heroes and heroines eat, drink, wear and drive a succession of carefully branded products. The public is now, for example, convinced that US *Top Gun* pilots wear 'Rayban' sunglasses simply because Tom Cruise wore them in the film, whereas in truth the USAF issues only 'Randolph' brand glasses.

At Wimbledon we see the players gratefully drinking their cups of Coca Cola and, at the Superbowl (the American football equivalent of the FA Cup final), swigging Gatorade. Both companies are eager to pay large sums for these testimonials. Another more subtle variant of this technique is the 'lending circuit' of jewels and *haute couture* fashions available freely to the famous, so that others (less so) may see them wearing these products and follow their example.

## The importance of marketing power

It is clear that these marketing techniques – market research, positioning strategy, advertising, direct marketing, conference management, design and brand association methods – are increasingly important to governments, political parties and businesses achieving their objectives. The British Government itself now spends annually over £167m both on communicating information on new legislation and reinforcing behavioural laws such as the drink-driving and seat-belt campaigns.

Before going to Central Office I was in charge of the D'Arcy, Masius, Benton and Bowles advertising team that produced the

DTI's £12m advertising campaign to make businesses aware of the Single European Market and it became clear to me then that, because we have a coming generation of politicians who are not only extremely adept at using the traditional skills of a politician, but also have marketing knowledge; the marketing of power by the powerful will become ever more sophisticated and significant. This does not mean, however, that it is – or ever will be – the most powerful method of creating images of power. There is a more powerful group still than the marketing experts. Bring on the 'news managers'.

# 4

# Managing the News

*Marx held that history is shaped by control of the
means of production; in our times history is
shaped by control of the means of communication.*

Arthur Schlesinger Jnr

This chapter is concerned with the nature of the news media, the
means whereby they can be controlled by the power élite and the
methods of image making that have been developed to create,
shape, restrict and manage the news.

## The emergence of the news managers

In the second half of the 20th century we have witnessed a
fundamental change in the power élite's ability to manage the
news. We are now living in a world where the news manager is
becoming as important to government and business as the
lawyers, accountants and administrators who inhabit the cor-
ridors outside the rooms where the decisions get made. The
powerful have an acute sense of survival and a highly developed
ability to sense danger. They realize that their enemies are now
organizing to destroy them by using the same techniques of
persuasion that they used to gain their power.

At one time governments and multinational corporations
were serenely indifferent to the mostly unprofessional, disor-
ganised and badly funded pressure groups that protested so
volubly outside their gates – until these groups started to hire
image makers for themselves. For example, even terrorists now

have their PROs. At the funeral of the IRA gunman Bobby Sands (who died on hunger strike), 300 camera operators and stills photographers recorded the event standing on a 25ft high scaffolding platform specially built for them by IRA public relations personnel.

Now the two sides face each other armed to the teeth with the latest hi-tech weapons of persuasion. The prize is public approval and the battleground is the media itself. When one realizes that the beneficial effects of expensive advertising campaigns can be wiped out by a single hostile news broadcast, it is obvious that it is those who shape the news who are the most powerful of all image makers.

Four quite distinct types of news manager have now emerged – all four functions may exceptionally be carried out by one person, but this is now rare as image makers tend to specialize. The first type manage the process of briefing the news media, eg press secretaries, spokespersons, spin doctors etc. Second, there are groups of image 'minders', eg advance men. Their function is both to make sure that the only pictures of their employers that are seen are the ones that present them in the best possible light and to arrange the smooth running of those occasions when the principal meets the media, like interviews, news conferences etc. Third, the powerful also employ 'wordsmiths', hired hands who provide them with their speeches, articles and *bons mots*. Lastly, there are those who attempt to shape media coverage, eg media and parliamentary lobbyists, public affairs advisers and crisis managers, by influencing those in the media and government with the power to make decisions.

These groups have been welded together by the power élite into an army capable not only of forming an impenetrable defensive square, but also of mounting a cavalry charge into enemy territory. The survival of entire governments and companies now depends on the effectiveness of these advisers, yet few outside the inner circles of power even know these mercenaries exist or what their true functions are.

In Chapter 1 I explained how, as big business grew to maturity and governments struggled against their enemies in war, both turned to the early public relations men like Lee and Bernays for help. In the same way that the contribution of women to the First World War effort made an extension of the franchise inevitable, so the company public relations managers and government information officers also claimed their reward: access to the powerful. What they gave the powerful in return was an understanding of the medium and how to control it.

## The word is power

In the beginning was the word and that word was power. Proprietors and editors from the Thunderer to Hearst's *New York Morning Journal* and Pulitzer's *New York World* wanted the power to influence events. Hearst and Pulitzer were so overcome by this urge that they ran for government office, while North-cliffe and Beaverbrook were given office by politicians who preferred to have them, in President Johnson's immortal phrase, (explaining his reasons for not sacking J Edgar Hoover) 'inside the tent pissing out, rather than outside pissing in'. During the 1930s Dawson, editor of *The Times* censored the dispatches of his own Berlin correspondents when he thought they would endanger the government's policy of appeasement. Similarly, in the early 1960s Dryfoos, the editor of the *New York Times*, censored his correspondents' reports of the preparations for the Bay of Pigs fiasco. Such is the corrupting influence of too close a relationship with the powerful.

In reality the press barons were much less of a success than their egos would allow them to admit. Rothermere's attacks on Baldwin were so foolishly conducted that the prime minister was probably saved by him from the justified wrath of the Tory party over unemployment. In fact, as Louis Heren has pointed out, it was the advertisers' muscle that really counted. When Rother-mere mounted a campaign in the *Daily Mail* in support of Oswald Mosley's blackshirts' violent forays into the East End centre of British Jewry, it was the manufacturers who advertised in the paper which forced him to drop his campaign.

And, while Beaverbrook ran the *Daily Express* as a vehicle for his particular brand of radical capitalism, he can hardly be said to have been successful in his campaigns to encourage Empire Free Trade (failed); save Edward VIII (failed), to stop rationing (failed), open an early Second Front (failed) or stop a Labour government being elected in 1945 (failed). Beaverbrook did succeed, however, in protecting the reputation of his friends. When F E Smith (later Lord Chancellor) was caught with a prostitute in Battersea Park and gave a false name to the police in the hope of evading scandal, Beaverbrook personally killed the story.

Baldwin's cutting personal opinion of Rothermere and Beaverbrook – 'they are both men that I would not have in my house', and his accusation (using his cousin Rudyard Kipling's phrase) that they had 'power without responsibility, the prerogative of the harlot throughout the ages' – are destined to be the press barons' epitaphs. Yet, very early on in the century the powerful recognized that they badly needed the press. The first US presidential press conference started as early as 1913, although it wasn't until Roosevelt took power in 1932 that they acquired the status of an art form. In Britain the General Strike prompted the government machine to investigate how it could control the news agenda better and in 1931 the first *de facto* No 10 press secretary, George Steward, appeared as Ramsay MacDonald's private secretary (intelligences) to service the ever growing power of the lobby.

## Television sound-bites

After the Second World War, television hijacked the relationship between the power élite and the media. In the US the first televised presidential press conference took place in 1953 and the first televised US cabinet meeting was in 1954 (the meeting was scripted by BBDO and cabinet members memorized their lines). In 1961 Pierre Salinger persuaded his boss John Kennedy to allow live news conferences and the US writing press started its long, slow decline into unpaid, bit-part players for the cameras. This in part was a reflection of the fact that people no longer looked to newspapers for news.

The process started first in the US, encouraged by the fact that there was no national newspaper. In 1951 the first coast-to-coast co-axial cable was laid, making live national news broadcast possible. A year later Walter Cronkite, the first TV 'anchorman', arrived on the screen. In 1963, Cronkite anchored the first half-hour news broadcast and by the end of that year, for the first time in history, research surveys showed that newspapers had been overtaken as the chief source of news. By 1980 the number of US households owning a television had reached the 80 million saturation point, Peter Dailey (Reagan's able media manager) could say in that year's election, without fear of contradiction. 'the evening news is the ball game, that's all there is to it'. Today, 65 per cent of Americans get 100 per cent of their news from television.

The pace of news gathering quickens every year. In 1968 the average sound-bite on US television in the election campaign was 42 seconds; by 1988 it had dropped to 10 seconds. This is partly explained by the audiences' growing ability to take in messages at great speed, partly by the networks' fear of boring their viewers (especially now the latter were armed with remote control devices) and partly because the image makers understood the medium much better than they had done in the 1950s.

## 'Hot' and 'cool' media

The most important influence on both the networks and the image makers was the Canadian academic Marshall McLuhan and his book *Understanding Media* (first published in 1964, but for a more sceptical view, see Jonathan Miller's analysis in *McLuhan*, Fontana, 1971). The theoretical basis of the book is an interesting (and still not bettered) attempt to define the nature of media by explaining that some – television, telephone, letters and cartoons – are 'cool', that is to say they communicate only a small amount of data and therefore encourage greater audience participation. Others – radio, movies, photographs, newspapers – are 'hot', that is to say they carry more data and that means lower participation. So far, so simple, but – perhaps because McLuhan was an academic and not a professional image maker – this theory has a very important practical consequence that the professor missed.

In order to restore control over the process of persuasion that television had diminished, it was first necessary for the image makers to develop an expertise both in understanding how to reduce this audience participation and finding methods of executing this reduction by increasing the amount of data that are supplied.

Take, for example, the modern televised speech. Every element that will appear on the screen is now considered beforehand by experts. The speaker's appearance (facial expression, clothes, body language), performance (humour, delivery, rhythm, pitch and tone) and environment (background, platform, surrounding colleagues, audience) is a body of data designed to persuade by excluding all other data. Technology (lighting, autocue, voice amplification and sound mixing) is used to invest this data with authority and to decrease the audience's participation. In the late 1940s Mrs Attlee would have driven the prime minister to a hall and he would take out some notes scribbled down on pieces of paper and deliver his speech. This would be dutifully reported without comment in the next day's newspapers. Today the prime minister's speech at the party conference, for example, takes a team of over fifty people to produce. All of these people are striving (just as a theatrical production team does) to flood the viewer with data and reduce audience participation.

The image makers have also taken McLuhan's warnings about the level of attention needed to understand television messages to heart. Compare the process of watching TV with that of a 'hot' medium like cinema. When we go to the movies we are consumed by light and sound. We dream rather than watch. Time seems irrelevant, belief is suspended and any distraction by the surrounding members of the audience is intensely irritating because it breaks this spell. There is no conscious need to concentrate. The nature of the medium is such that we are in its grip until the house lights come up. Contrast this with the process of watching television. Here we have a sense of control and distance (what Brecht was searching for in his '*Verfremdungseffekt*', or alienation effect). We can change the picture, colour and sound at will. We can tune out the voices we hear and contemplate the appearance and manner of the person speaking. Other people in the room talk, read, eat and make a variety of distracting noises in a way that would be maddening in the cinema. Our level of interest waxes and wanes. If you appear on television you will find that people can easily remember what you looked like, but very little of what you said. Appear, if that's the right expression, on the radio and what you say and how you say it are easily remembered. The obvious conclusion of this is that it is not only extremely difficult to get your message across and remembered on television, but it is also difficult to achieve this without other unwanted messages also being transmitted.

## The briefers

Understanding the nature of the medium led to a desire to control it, and by the 1960s the powerful had institutionalized the role of the 'briefer', partly to restrict access to themselves and partly to build a relationship with the media that they had neither the time, expertise nor inclination to build.

The chief tasks of the briefers are to be the public voice of the principal; to fill in the background facts; to provide a context for the events and issues of the day; to correct misconceptions and factual errors; and to act as a liaison for media 'bids' (eg requests for interviews etc).

To practise the first of these, both formal mechanisms and informal relationships have to be constructed. In Britain, the lobby system has developed to provide a forum where the briefers can answer journalists' questions or where politicians themselves may talk to the media unattributably.

What are perhaps most interesting to analyze are the informal relationships between briefers and the media. Sir Bernard Ingham emphasizes the importance of this when he says that his 'greatest single achievement was maintaining relations with the media'. He knew that Mrs Thatcher was not interested in the media (except for a few friends to whom she spoke regularly, like Woodrow Wyatt), because she believed that if one got the policy right it would virtually present itself, and also because she was secretive both by nature and by training. This meant that how the policy was to be presented was rarely, if ever, built into the planning phase of policy creation. The result of all this was that Ingham felt he had to redress the balance both by taking the initiative with the media and by representing them in government (as he did in 1982 when he forced the Ministry of Defence to allow journalists to sail with the Falklands Task Force).

Ingham was unusually close to his boss and journalists soon realized that when they asked him a question it was nearly as good as asking her. Nearly, but not always. Indeed, Michael

Jones (of the *Sunday Times*) tells the story of once meeting Mrs Thatcher and Ingham by chance. The prime minister challenged his account in the previous Sunday's paper of her supposed views. Nervously, Jones looked to Ingham for reassurance and said, 'but that was the line, wasn't it, Bernard?'. Sensing what had happened, Mrs Thatcher grinned and said (looking hard at her press secretary), 'Well Michael, I didn't know I thought that until I read it in your column.' As Ingham says himself, his job was 'to preserve credibility without lying'. His credibility was such that he was largely responsible for the media believing that we would use the Falklands Task force if we had to and that the government would not give in to the miners in 1984. In both cases, the media's initial scepticism of the government's determination disappeared after repeated helpings of Ingham's robust and sometimes even aggressive briefings. In 1982 he asked one journalist, 'Why do you think we are sending 25,000 people south? For the joy of the journey?'. He was equally convincing when he explained to doubting Thomases that the stockpiling of coal was carried out specifically to withstand the predicted strike for a lengthy period.

However, Ingham's personality also unintentionally played an important part in the media's perception of Mrs Thatcher in ways that were sometimes not always good for her image. When, for example, he used one of his favourite Yorkshire expressions like 'she's not best pleased', lobby journalists tended to translate this into 'she is chewing the carpet and foaming at the mouth' – without it necessarily being a true reflection of her feelings.

So, what constitutes a good briefer? Well, good briefers don't lie, rather, they omit that part of the truth that will harm their principal.

– They understand both the facts of the matter and their principal's attitudes to those facts.

– They are utterly loyal to their principal (and receive loyalty in return).

– They know when to respond and are always available to respond.

– They maintain an open-door policy, even to those journalists whose interests are inimical to theirs.

- They do not attempt to create policy, but are frank in their advice to their principal if they believe that the policy is defective.

- They have a finely developed sense of humour.

- They are firm, but courteous with the media.

- They stay in the shadows where they belong and do not seek publicity for themselves.

- They are clear, articulate, convincing in arguments, self-confident and literate.

- They are good listeners and know when to ask rather than to tell.

- They must be able to spot what the media will see in a story and understand how different sections of the media will treat a story.

- They are interested in the news-gathering process and understand the working lives, problems and anxieties of journalists.

- They are single-minded and disciplined in the way they identify the key point they wish to communicate.

- They are interested in the history of communications and study past techniques.

- They monitor the media's output obsessively and are good judges of what makes a story truly important.

- They like and/or admire their principal, but have a realistic view of his or her weaknesses.

- They are calm and unflappable in a crisis.

- They possess the gift of objectivity and a sense of proportion.

- They have thick skins, as they will inevitably be the target of those with power, no responsibility – and a score to settle.

- They know instinctively when to complain and when to leave well alone.

- They need the constitution of an ox, the digestion of a goat and the stamina of a marathon runner!

Gennadi Gerasimov, who was Gorbachev's briefer, once gave me his own definition of the qualities required of the super briefer. 'A good spokesman', he said, 'should possess several admirable qualities. He should be tolerant of repetitive questions and never lose his temper, have a self-deprecatory sense of humour and never take himself too seriously, and be ready to see his wife only at night and his girlfriends only occasionally.

It is worth remembering Eisenhower's advice to a thin-skinned friend. 'This paper is not very widely read. Of those who read it, half will not read this story. Of those who read this story, half will not understand what the writer is driving at. Of those who will understand it, half will not believe it. Of those who believe it, half will be people whose opinion means nothing whatsoever. So why are you worrying?'.

## Spin doctoring

*God is in the details*

Mies van der Rohe

One increasingly important task of the briefer is to seek to ensure that the correct line is picked up by the media. This activity is known as spin doctoring. Although lazy journalists sometimes use the term carelessly to refer to any image maker, it has in fact a very specialized meaning. The concept was invented in the US and developed originally as part of the process whereby the briefers fought to claim victory in the Ford–Carter debates.

As Larry Speakes (Reagan's press secretary) recalls in his memoirs, every news manager in the US had learnt the same lesson from these debates, which was 'he who claimed victory *first* was the winner'. At that time, Speakes was working for Ford's vice-presidential nominee, Robert Dole, and he was worried that his principal's mean streak would show in the up-coming debate with Mondale. Speakes went to work to see if he could mount a 'spin patrol' so complete that it would guarantee victory. He arranged with ABC, CBS and NBC that Elizabeth Dole, John Connally and Vice-President Rockefeller would leave their front-row seats immediately the debate ended and go straight to a preassigned live camera for a down-the-line *post mortem*. Each one claimed victory on all three networks, so Speakes had nine positive 'at bats' before Mondale's supporters were even on-air.

Dole, meanwhile, left the rostrum and quickly went to an adjoining room, where, again on live television, he received a prearranged telephone call of congratulation from President Ford. Speakes then obtained the campaign's instant feedback polling data which showed Dole to be ahead and released it to the waiting media. It was all to no avail. Dole had said in the debate that both World Wars, Korea and Vietnam had all been 'Democratic wars' (ie had been started when the Democrats ran congress). The media promptly interpreted Dole's statement as a smear that Democrats purposely started wars. Mondale quickly picked this up and ran with it, so that at the end of the post-debate day the media were acclaiming Mondale the winner. However, Speakes developed spin doctoring from this early experience and used it very successfully in post-summit briefings, especially when he turned the Reagan–Gorbachev Reykjavik meeting into a personal triumph for the US president.

Since then spin doctoring has been commonly used in Britain for example after important speeches. The spin patrols haunt the press room at party conferences helpfully pointing out key passages and significant phrases to journalists hard pressed to deliver their copy. To help the television reporters copies of the speeches are supplied with suggestions as to which passages should be selected for airing.

The power of the spin patrol was well illustrated after the Maastricht summit in December 1991, when the Government's delaying tactics over economic and monetary union were parlayed into a diplomatic triumph for John Major by a team of government and party spin doctors.

There are many variations on the basic technique. Here are two from my own diaries. The first is an example of spin doctoring to manage expectations (an old news managers' technique) prior to the event and the other is an example of correcting a problem after an interview that's gone wrong.

In February 1990 I received a paper from Tony Kerpel, Kenneth Baker's political adviser and one of the sharper minds in British politics. In his memo Tony warned us that the greatest test for the party that year would be the local government elections, to be held on 3 May. The Conservatives had been outfought by Labour in the 1989 European Parliament elections. The leadership challenge of Sir Anthony Meyer had been more serious than people realized, and the mounting rows over the poll tax, together with doubts over economic policy, meant that we were losing by-elections. Labour's momentum was building all the time and the May local government elections, which the party normally treated as a secondary event, were the only opportunity to both stop Labour's rise in the polls and to consolidate Mrs Thatcher's position. We therefore needed to fight a high-profile national campaign to demonstrate that Central Office was still an effective election machine.

I asked the psephological experts inside Central Office what their projection was for May. Their answer (shorn of all the statistics and health warnings) was that it would be a rout. They did say, however, that the swing to Labour would not be uniform and that the results in Westminster, Wandsworth and Bradford might be better than the national picture if professional and determined campaigns took place.

Tony had made the point in his paper that we couldn't avoid the poll tax being the main issue and that if we didn't defend it with everything at our disposal then we couldn't expect either the party or the voters to have much faith in it. We decided to find the money for an advertising campaign that would tackle the opposition to the tax head on and Tim Bell and I went to work on a communications strategy.

We agreed on three main points. First, that the principle of the tax might be accepted eventually, but only if people accepted that it was based on fairness (before all candidates in the Tory leadership contest announced they would scrap the tax, opinion polls showed 40 per cent in favour of the principle behind it, namely that everyone should pay something towards the cost of local government. Second, that the real problem was the amount people had to pay. Third, that if we could prove that it was only under Labour-run councils that the charge was high, then we could rehearse one of our preferred general election themes: 'Labour costs you more'.

We therefore took the gamble that in those few Tory councils with a very low poll tax, we would win the local election campaigns. I then started to brief the media that we would consider ourselves the victors if that happened, irrespective of Labour gains elsewhere. This 'ante' spin doctoring worked very well and by the end of the campaign the media were all repeating the line that if the Tories were to hold Westminster, Wandsworth (and perhaps Bradford), then the poll tax furore would probably die down; doubts over Mrs Thatcher's leadership would subside, and Labour's momentum would be stopped in its tracks.

During the election we pulled out all the campaigning stops. Our ads were far superior to Labour's indifferent and poorly funded efforts, and we came up with some excellent photo opportunities to illustrate the campaign theme that 'Labour councils cost you more'.

By the early morning of 4 May it was clear that the spin patrol strategy had worked. We won the elections in Westminster and Wandsworth, actually increasing the number of our seats and confounding the pollsters. Although Labour protested loudly that they had won the election nationally (which of course was perfectly true), the media were reporting that Tory prospects had not looked brighter for many months. We immediately decided to accept all media bids. After a few hours' sleep, party chairman Kenneth Baker and I headed off to the television and radio studios for a heavy round of interviews in which he stoutly maintained the line that 'our victory' proved that the principle of the poll tax was being accepted and that where the tax was low enough then people would vote for it.

In the car returning to Central Office the phone rang and I was told that there were several television crews outside the front door to film the comings and goings. I pulled out from my pile of newspapers a copy of the *Sun* with its enormous 'KINNOCK POLL AXED' front-page headline and gave it to Kenneth Baker, suggesting that he should hold it up in front of him when he got out of the car. The headline and his smiling face on the evening news would, I thought, underline the spin. To the ordinary viewer the impression would be that the Tories were feeling pretty pleased with themselves at this turnaround in their fortunes.

The cameras were then invited in to film the chairman congratulating the staff on all their efforts. I was then astounded to learn from the BBC that the Labour team had refused to appear live on the lunchtime news as they had gone to bed. So, I jumped at another chance for a free ride and we had yet another opportunity to announce our victory, this time with no Labour spokesperson to contradict us (or give out the inconvenient statistics of Labour gains).

The final act of the spin patrol was to book a table for Kenneth, myself and Central Office staff to lunch on the terrace of the House of Commons where the political correspondents congregate in summer. We celebrated our victory in grand style and, by the end of lunch, most of the reporters from the Sunday papers had wandered over for a chat.

That night's television news and the following day's press were a director of communications' dream come true. Heseltine's ambition to exploit a Tory defeat had been abruptly terminated; the prime minister's position was strengthened; backbench morale improved; the polls reported that we had cut Labour's lead by 7 percentage points; the poll tax argument had been shifted from one of principle to the size of the bill, and Central Office had proved that it could out-campaign Labour.

A more usual kind of spin patrol is exemplified by an incident which happened late in 1989. At the weekend following Nigel Lawson's resignation there was intense press speculation about party morale. We decided on Monday morning that the party chairman would accept bids from ITN and BBC News for pre-records to make the point that economic policy was not affected by Mr Lawson's departure and to generally calm things down.

That lunchtime Mrs Thatcher entertained the 1922 Committee of senior backbenchers, together with selected cabinet ministers. After lunch I received a telephone call from Charles Reiss, the *Evening Standard*'s energetic political editor, to say that rumours were flying about Whitehall that the backbenchers had been critical over lunch of Mrs Thatcher's performance. The phrase 'You must get your act together' was allegedly used to her face. This, together with rumours of a challenge to Mrs Thatcher's leadership, was raising the Whitehall temperature to fever pitch. Although I didn't know anyone on the committee who was stupid (or courageous) enough to say such a thing, I quickly checked with someone who had been present, who confirmed that no such statement had been made. As we walked over to St Stephen's Green, where Michael Brunson of ITN was waiting, I briefed Kenneth Baker and reminded him that he should not discuss the lunchtime session, as it was a private meeting.

Predictably, Brunson had abandoned the list of questions that he had been planning to ask before lunch and went straight to the nub of the matter. Did they really say that to the prime minister? At this Kenneth hesitated and honestly admitted that something of the sort had been mentioned. It was not aimed at the PM, more at the government as a whole. Too late did he see my warning frown and Brunson's beaming face.

The papers next day told the story. *The Times* reported 'Top Tories warn Thatcher'.

Puzzled, I tackled Kenneth on why he had confirmed the story when no one had in fact used those words. He said in protest, 'But they had', which was even more puzzling, as they had not. Over the next few days stories abounded in the press of the cabinet's supposed disloyalty to the prime minister (a ridiculous assertion in Baker's case as he was, always, entirely loyal). We did our best to squash speculation, while I tried to solve the mystery of who said what to whom.

A successful spin patrol was mounted to convince the lobby that no backbench revolt existed and there was no disloyalty from Baker. Yet in her *Panorama* interview following the Queen's Speech the prime minister was again asked what had been said to her by the 1922 Committee. By now I had found out the truth. One of the committee members, in the grip of a boastful fantasy, had told Kenneth (and the media) that he had used the offending phrase, when in fact he had not.

The spin patrol went on the march again that afternoon, this time with more success. 'Baker moves to defuse Thatcher lunch doubt', said *The Times*. After this the stories of disloyalty faded away and the Meyer challenge passed off uneventfully.

These two examples show first how difficult it is to kill off a rumour once it has started, especially when most of the people involved have a vested interest in keeping the rumour afloat; second that spin doctoring needs the persistence of Robert the Bruce's spider; and third that spin doctoring is a flexible technique that can be used not only to 'fix' the results of events (speeches, interviews, debates and so on) after the event, but also to manage the expectations of an event yet to take place. Indeed, some of the most successful spin patrols we ever mounted followed Kinnock's set-piece television interviews, briefing the press on the 'mistakes' he had made.

## Leaking

James Callaghan said, 'You know the difference between leaking and briefing. Leaking is what you do, briefing is what I do.'

Leaking is an occupational hazard for news managers and is famously difficult to deal with effectively. It is a traditional weapon in internecine Whitehall battles, for example, at the start of the Gulf War, MI6 leaked the fact that MI5 had interned Iraqis and Palestinians on the basis of inaccurate records. MI6 is keen to take over some of MI5's jurisdiction, particularly terrorism and Northern Ireland.

Victorian cabinet ministers used to leak the results of their discussions to J T Delane of *The Times* and in the Edwardian era Admiral Fisher deliberately leaked Cabinet secrets to J L Garvin of the *Observer* in order to affect the outcome of the 1908 naval rearmament debate. In modern times Sir Stafford Cripps's wife leaked all the 1945 Labour government's discussions to Hugh Massingham of the *Observer* over tea every Friday afternoon, while Rab Butler and George Brown were notorious leakers (the former leaked the whole story of Macmillan's 'night of the long knives' reshuffle to the *Daily Mail*). But it was Harold Wilson who made it a deliberate policy, using (so Crossman claimed in his diaries) Gerald Kaufman and George Wigg to do the dirty work. However, as Sir John Junor (former editor of the *Sunday Express*) observed in his memoirs, Wilson was not above leaking direct.

Junor tells the story in which Wilson once read an article in which it was claimed he was planning to sack all junior ministers over 52. On reading it Wilson idly wondered who the source was for the story and then suddenly remembered he had leaked it himself!

Wilson's press secretary, Joe Haines, regularly received intelligence from a Tory MP (who wanted Wilson to grant him an honour), and while it usually turned out to be low-grade material there is some evidence that his information about Tory campaign plans persuaded Wilson to call an early election in 1970.

I occasionally received the same sort of leaking from Labour party sources but, as the saying goes, 'knowing that it's going to rain does not stop it raining'. However, leaking from Central Office was drastically reduced after a computerised telephone exchange was installed, which could catch leakers by simply matching up calls made from the office to an extensive list of telephone numbers belonging to journalists. The Thatcher cabinet was very leaky, not only about confidential policy matters, but also in the form of indiscreet or consciously malevolent remarks about each other made over lunch with lobby journalists.

Most leakers are motivated by a desire to feel important or to ingratiate themselves with reporters. However, some leaks are carried out to shape policy (by flying a kite and seeing the reaction it gets) or to kill a policy off. Briefers do leak on occasion themselves; for example, privately commissioned opinion polls that are favourable to a party are routinely leaked by them to bolster their postion, and to try and create that most valuable of all political commodities, momentum.

Central Office had a campaign before the 1987 election of leaking items that could be an embarrassment in the election campaign itself, eg the fact that the chairperson of one of the London constituency parties had some years before been a National Front member. As Bernard Ingham discovered to his chagrin, even the deliberations of his own committee to co-ordinate government presentation (M10) leaked.

## Shaping the news

In general, it is an entirely different group of news managers who trade in confidential information. These are what may be called 'influencers', whose job is to influence those in the media and others with the power to form opinion. This group often clashes with the briefers (as the long history of enmity between Messrs Bell and Ingham shows), because their relationships with the powerful are informal and hidden from view.

Influencers come in two basic forms: media lobbyists, who are paid to influence journalists about the merits of a particular interest; and parliamentary lobbyists, who have politicians, civil servants and others in or near government as their target.

### *Media lobbyists*

The true successors of Ivy Lee and Bernays are the media

lobbyists of today. In the same way that the former came to prominence as defenders of the robber barons against the first muck-raking, anti-trust journalists, the media lobbyists were a reaction to the consumerism of the 1960s. After Ralph Nader's successful 'whistle-blowing' campaigns against General Motors (which led to car safety legislation), many companies realised that quite small but enthusiastic groups like 'Nader's Raiders' could attract the interest of the media, who were themselves keen to show off their consumerist credentials. Mostly, these pressure groups tend to be negative in nature (eg anti-smoking or anti-blood sports) which makes for better news value, and the few that are constructive (eg SAVE the conservationist cam-paingners) can easily get ignored unless they take an aggressively anti-Establishment stance.

Other clients of the media lobbyist include foreign govern-ments; companies in the throes of being merged, taken over or who wish to contest bids; and those who find themselves in the midst of a crisis, eg resignations, product failure, major accident, strikes or scandal.

*Crisis managers*

When Perrier discovered small traces of benzene in its bottled water and when Johnson & Johnson's Tylenol was tainted by cyanide in a criminal conspiracy, these experts were on hand to deal with the crisis and mount successful campaigns to rehabili-tate the brands' image with the consumer. For example, the Perrier crisis was managed in the UK by a four-person team (presciently set up five years earlier), which included an execu-tive of Infoplan, the PR agency. Source Perrier in Paris were totally unprepared. The chairman and founder of the company was subsequently replaced.

When a British Midland aircraft crashed in 1989 with 44 fatalities, a potentially disastrous loss of confidence was averted by the skilful pre-planning of a crisis strategy by their PR agency and the outstandingly impressive news management skills of British Midland's Chairman Sir Michael Bishop. During the miners' strike of 1985, the NCB brought in both Tim Bell and Sir Gordon Reece to mastermind the board's PR and advertising strategy which ultimately led to a humiliating defeat for the

NUM (and, in the process, revolutionized the TUC's attitude to the use of image makers). When Sir Ralph Halpern, chairman of Burton, was discovered in an adulterous relationship with a young girl (and attempts to blackmail him were being made by a third party), it was Bell yet again who handled the crisis in such a way as to ensure that Halpern remained in his post.

## Foreign clients

Media lobbyists have always worked on behalf of foreign countries, but this trend is accelerating. For example, Bell's company now works for such diverse interests as Malaysia, Brunei, Abu Dhabi and the Republic of Kazakhstan, while the People's Republic of China is represented by Hill and Knowlton, and the impressively conducted Free Kuwait Campaign during the Gulf War was run by GJW.

## PR and business mega-bids

Contested bids like the bitter Guinness takeover, or the failed Goldsmith bid for BAT, are now carried out by crisis teams of PR advisers rather than accountants and lawyers. Hanson, one of the most successful at acquisitions, not only hired Michael Shea (the Queen's longest-serving press secretary), but also put on retainer Tim Bell, Brian Basham and Roddy Dewe. This trio could claim to be three of the most experienced crisis managers in the City, who are highly skilled at the often vicious in-fighting that accompanies mega-bids. Indeed, Shea (a Scot) was recently appointed visiting professor at Strathclyde University Graduate Business School in 1991, which is clear evidence that the sleepy groves of academe are finally waking up to the existence of this enormously influential group in society which has hardly been the subject of any proper academic study at all.

Such advisers have two basic modes of operation, each based on adapting a standard theory of communications. The 'consonance and dissonance' approach is commonly used when trying to change attitudes. It can be explained by using the arguments over smoking as an example. A state of consonance in this context would be 'I smoke and I'm perfectly happy smoking'. A state of dissonance would be 'I smoke and I know it's going to kill me'. What the anti-smoking lobbyists aim to do is shut the dissonant smoker off from escape routes, eg 'My father smoked and he lived to win the London Marathon at 85' or 'What's the point in giving up as I could be run over by a bus tomorrow?'. When all the escape routes are shut off, then the dissonant smoker has been manoeuvred into the position where giving up tobacco is probably inevitable.

This same technique is used against floating voters – who, by the very fact they have not made up their minds, are obviously dissonant. The others are loyal to one of the parties (or consonant) and normally won't change their minds.

The 'latitude of acceptance' theory posits that an identical message from two different sources has two different effects. To continue the smoking example, if a tramp approaches you in a coughing fit and asks for a cigarette, claiming that there's nothing better for one's health and longevity than smoking tobacco, you are not likely to be impressed with his argument. If, however, the College of Surgeons releases new research stating categorically that there's nothing better for one's health and longevity than smoking cigarettes, one is apt to have one's existing attitudes to tobacco challenged.

The lobbyists, therefore, proceed on the basis that either they should admit their bias to the media frankly ('You know I represent BAT, but ...'), which can be very effective, or they have to introduce an objective testimonial into the discussion, which is why opinion polling is used so often to 'objectify' the arguments the lobbyist is using.

Public relations is in essence built on the introduction of third party endorsement into the debate in an effort to achieve credibility. These endorsements come from a descending hierarchy of authority figures delivering messages through a descending hierarchy of media. For example, at the top is the word of mouth recommendation by your own doctor of a medicine. This is more convincing than the words of a doctor you don't know, in a newspaper article. That in turn is more effective than a doctor in an advertisement. All of these are better than the views of the Archbishop of Canterbury, which in turn are more persuasive than, say, a quiz show host, and so on.

Media lobbyists have very close connections with the other main group of news managers, the parliamentary lobbyist.

## *Parliamentary lobbyists*

Business leaders are surprisingly unfamiliar with Whitehall and its ways. Indeed, one of Britain's leading lobbyists, Ian Greer (who was John Major's chauffeur in the Tory party leadership contest), estimates that 90 per cent of those coming to him for help (usually, he says, too late in the day) have never met the relevant permanent secretary or had any closer contact with the secretary of state at the appropriate department than sitting next to them at an industry lunch. White Papers quite often come as a complete shock to business leaders and it is often the case that only a Bill's appearance will shake them into taking action, which is when the parliamentary lobbyists are hired.

Legislation is examined minutely by the lobbyist so that the consequences for their client's business are fully understood. The client is given an initial assessment of the chances of getting changes made in the Bill. These may be slight if the measure had an ideological base, which means that the government is highly unlikely to be moved from its chosen course. The team then start to make calls to ministers and to other politicians and their advisers on the relevant select or backbench committees to request a meeting (usually over lunch or a drink) to find out how the land lies. Politicians of all parties usually know senior lobbyists well and a great deal of trust will have been built up over a period of time, so they are likely to accept these invitations. The team also talks to the departmental officials concerned (normally above the rank of assistant secretary), but on a more formal basis.

Both groups have an interest in seeing that legislation does not get into trouble as it goes through parliament. The civil servants have an interest, as it is they who draft laws. The politicians have because any embarrassment could be exploited by opposition parties. Lobbyists in these meetings often take into account the latitude of acceptance theory, by straightforwardly explaining that, although they are evidently partial, they see deficiencies in the Bill which could cause either politicians, or their officials, harm at a later date.

A strategy to influence the legislation is then created from these discussions, which normally includes recommendations on what methods of persuasion should be used, eg advertising, direct mail etc. The key to success for the lobbyist is to try and get a group of people on their side, people who have access to, or influence on, the secretary of state. These will mainly be backbenchers, but also the minister's parliamentary private secretary and his special adviser, plus any appropriate junior ministers. Meetings would be arranged for the client to present views to key members of the decision-making unit, and advice is given by the lobbyist on what should be said in these presentations and how the points should be made to particular personalities. Specialist reporters and lobby correspondents are then briefed on the facts of the client's case.

Both these groups of journalists will be offered (by both sides of the argument) various blandishments, particularly overseas travel and other forms of entertainment that they might not otherwise be able to afford, and this is what has led to calls for a US-style register of lobbyists' clients.

During this time the lobbyists are giving constant intelligence and feedback to their clients on how the campaign is progressing as the legislation moves through the various stages of the parliamentary process, especially the committee and report stages.

In essence, lobbyists have a symbiotic relationship with the powerful, acting as they do as both expert political advisers and as brokers between industry and government. They have made an important and often hidden contribution to causes such as the anti-Sunday trading campaign (when a Bill was defeated by the lobbyists pressurizing constituency MPs) and to the management of contested bids (eg the Barclay brothers' bid for Calor Gas which was destroyed by lobbyists engineering a reference to the Monopolies Commission. They have also successfully mounted campaigns of opposition to government policies, such as the Ridley proposals to give BA's American and Far East routes to BCal or the brewers' campaign to oppose Lord Young's policy to provide greater competition in the pub trade.

The combination of media and parliamentary lobbyists is a very powerful one and there are more and more examples of the powerful achieving their objectives without recourse to any other form of image maker than these two groups of news managers.

# The rise of the 'minders'

The rise of the news manager over the last 30 years is (at least partly) explained by a need to counter both the power and the perceived bias of the media. The press has a long history of skulduggery from the 1925 Zinoviev letter in the *Daily Mail*; to the *Daily Express* headline branding the Labour 1945 election victory 'National Socialist'; and the *Daily Mirror* front page before the 1951 election asking 'Whose finger on the trigger?', which implied that Churchill was a warmonger (Churchill sued and won).

In the US, during the 1928 election, one newspaper showed Al Smith (who was a Catholic) standing next to the entrance to the newly dedicated New York Holland tunnel roadway. The caption helpfully explained that this was the tunnel linking the White House to the Vatican. Some papers in 1960 similarly reported the (forged) Kennedy slogan, 'The Virgin Mary will be the First Lady'. These, however, were cases of institutionalized bias that had gone over the top. Both parties accepted that newspapers were biased and outside of the kind of 'up to no good boyo' antics described above, proprietorial prejudice or editorial bile was simply treated as part of the rough and tumble of political life. Indeed, the 'Tory' press is not the monolith of myth. The 'anti-Labour' press would be a more apt description.

In 1940, Roosevelt had won the election with only 21 per cent of the daily papers supporting him, so politicians knew it was not necessarily critical to victory. It wasn't until television had truly established itself in the 1960s that the relationship between government and media got into today's parlous state of antipathy and distrust. Although senior television executives make a religion out of impartiality (with some success: 70 per cent of viewers think the BBC is not biased), some of their staff can fall from grace occasionally and a very small minority are practising atheists!

Outsiders should understand that most politicians, although they put a brave face on it, are extremely thin-skinned and privately think that all journalists are professional 'shits' (their word, not mine) and, deep down, most journalists agree with H L Mencken that their relationship to a politician should be that of dog to lamp-post. In my view, all journalists are trustworthy – until proven guilty.

If a politicain suspects political bias on top of personal prejudice, then the stage is usually set for a very ugly confrontation.

## The revolution in broadcast journalism

Although the Macmillan government's relationship with the media suffered at the hands of television satirists, the rot really started with Harold Wilson. Ironically, given what was to come, Wilson started out in opposition with the objective that television should be wooed assiduously to counter the effects of the 'Tory press'. When in power the Labour prime minister decided that he would take Roosevelt's fireside chats as his broadcasting model.

The BBC, however, had other ideas. They had changed the old system of ministerial broadcasts (giving equal time to government and opposition) to a scheme whereby the BBC issued 'invitations' to the prime minister of the day and then decided, on the basis of his talk, whether or not to invite the leader of the opposition to speak. Wilson's desire to appear on television every other week soon led to a clash of wills, which the BBC won. The lingering resentment Wilson felt impelled him to set up a media monitoring unit at Transport House (the party HQ), to comb the airwaves for examples of anti-government bias. The politician's traditional paranoia was beginning to turn into something more deeply felt.

What was happening during this time was nothing less than a revolution in broadcast journalism. The automatic forelock-tugging respect that prime ministers had previously enjoyed had disappeared. David Frost built on Robin Day's forensic interviewing techniques to produce the 'trial by television' interview, eg the public crucifixion of the swindler Emil Savundra. The cosy relationships between politicians and journalists were breaking down and interviewers could no longer be relied upon to stick to a pre-agreed agenda.

For any Labour government, the idea that the BBC and ITN might contain powerful individuals who were anti-Labour was a particularly frightening thought, as they could count on only a handful of newspapers to support them. Wilson tried every method he could think of to bring the BBC to heel, threatening them with Tony Wedgwood Benn's plan for introducing advertising, while at the same time refusing to raise the licence fee. Finally Wilson hit upon what he thought was a master stroke: he appointed a politician, Lord Hill, the former cabinet minister, to keep the BBC in order. Unfortunately, as so often happens, Hill went native and backed the broadcasters in every wearisome dispute with the Corporation.

Wilson's distrust (increasingly matched by Heath's, who, during this period, called the BBC's director-general a liar and promised him that when in power he would break the tyranny of the BBC) started to get out of hand. He insisted that Radio 1 disc jockeys were secretly anti-Labour. When David Dimbleby's commentary on Nixon's 1969 Chequers visit strayed into the satiric (he noted Nixon's 'face for all seasons' and the 'expensively hired press secretaries, whose job is to disguise the truth'), a huge row ensued and the BBC was quickly forced to apologise.

After the 1970 election Dimbleby followed this irresponsible exploitation of free speech to make a *24 Hours* programme that, in the politician's encyclopedia of BBC demonology, has a very long entry. It is a programme that every image maker since has studied carefully as it is the paradigm of a genre known as the 'stitch-up'. The format was simple. First, Dimbleby and his colleagues shot some seemingly innocent footage of Wilson with his agreement. There was Wilson playing golf, leading the singing in a pub, reading a lesson in church (the vicar refused to use 2 Samuel i 19 as a text – 'How are the mighty fallen') and generally behaving in a carefree and respectable fashion. Dimbleby then interviewed Wilson in his room in the Commons. To Wilson's fury, Dimbleby then asked him whether the £250,000 earnings from his memoirs were a consolation for losing office. Wilson exploded and demanded that the filming be stopped and this passage deleted. Predictably the story leaked (the BBC is expert at protecting itself this way), and Wilson threatened libel writs and an injunction. After prising the only copy of the film from under the producer's grip (she was convinced that if she slept with it under her pillow no one could cut it without her knowing), the BBC governors watched the finished version and gave their permission for it to be shown.

*Yesterday's Men*, as the programme was called (an ironic reference to the headline of an anti-Tory ad in the election), was the perfect stitch-up. Everyone in it was portrayed as venal and without scruples. Satirical songs and cartoons by Gerald Scarfe had been commissioned to mock the interviewees, who, it goes without saying, had not been told what the format of the film would be. The internal BBC enquiry whitewashed the producers, although Huw Weldon later observed that the programme was like 'making a film about family doctors, with their co-operation, and then calling it *Quack Quack'*.

From that day on, any lingering trust that might have existed between broadcasters and the powerful disappeared, and a new breed of image maker was commissioned to protect them from the broadcasters' destructive power: the 'minder'. This is not to say that the media is the image makers' enemy; indeed they are often friendly allies. The best analogy of the relationship is that they are like opponents in a game of chess. These minders devised two principal methods of ensuring the right kind of media coverage. First, they arranged that the principal be increasingly seen by the public without reporters being involved, and secondly, if an interview was necessary (and from now on *they* would decide if it was), then *they* would negotiate the terms and devise ways for hostile questions to be avoided or dealt with satisfactorily.

The first of these methods came in two basic variants: the photo-opportunity and its near relation, the walkabout.

### 'Pseudo events'

Daniel Boorstin first analyzed this new media phenomenon in his seminal book *The Image* (published in 1962) and he defined what he called these 'pseudo events' as unspontaneous, newsworthy and ambiguous in their relation to reality. He pointed out that the public relations expert 'not only knows what news value is, but, knowing it, he is in a position to make news happen. He is a creator of events.' Boorstin was exactly right when he paraphrased Gresham's Law to describe photo-opportunites as 'counterfeit happenings which tend to drive spontaneous happenings out of circulation'. They are usually deliberate and conscious attempts by the image makers to create news, using methods made possible by the new video technology.

In the 1970s, election coverage in Britain consisted largely of outside broadcast (OB) coverage of the parties' morning press conferences, using large, heavy and unwieldy television cameras. The same OB cameras were also sent to cover the evening speeches which were recorded on large spool videotape. Sixteen mm cameras were used on tripods to record the leaders on the campaign trail. The film had to be processed in a huge 'bath' for up to an hour, then edited on a viewing machine and the voice-over dubbed in the studio.

In March 1978 a former television director arrived at Conservative Central Office to take up the post of director of publicity. Gordon (later Sir Gordon) Reece decided that Mrs Thatcher's campaigning should be timetabled around the needs of the television news. He knew that the most vital communications target in modern elections is the skilled working class ($C_2$s in socio-economic terms) and these voters mostly watched the early evening news, both national and regional. Reece devised a scheme whereby the events he wanted to feature in the news took place in time for the film to be processed and then broadcast.

Reece was experienced enough in television methods to know that the news editors would fall over themselves to use any interesting visuals they were given, so he prepared a daily series of 'events', each one of which was carefully designed to highlight a different aspect of Mrs Thatcher's personality. This was, in Michael White's phrase, 'televison with the sound turned down'. Viewers saw her tasting tea in Newcastle, having her heartbeat tested electronically in Milton Keynes, sewing ladies' clothes in Leicester and, most famously of all, cuddling a new-born calf in a field at Eye.

Mrs Thatcher herself was responsible for the invention of the 'no photos' photo opportunity. One day she climbed up the side of a factory chimney with the cameras following her progress. Half-way up she froze suddenly, realizing the consequences of a woman ascending wearing a skirt. 'Don't look', she said sternly, and all eyes (and cameras) were sheepishly lowered. Complaints from the accompanying reporters that these were just 'media events' did not impress their own editors, who were fascinated by the pictures they were receiving from the campaign trail.

In the early 1980s the news-gathering process was revolutionized by the development of lightweight video cameras that recorded (from available light) pictures on to book-sized videotape cassettes and sent them down a special line (or by satellite transmitter) to the broadcasting company's headquarters.

Although plans were made to use these Electronic News Gathering (ENG) cameras in the Falklands, the Ministry of Defence banned all transmissions from the islands (fearing a Vietnam-style domestic reaction) and the tapes had to be sent on passing ships to Ascension Island. The result was that the public saw pictures days, sometimes even weeks, old.

So it wasn't until the 1983 election that ENG's capacities for speed and flexibility were fully realized. This time Reece's concept was treated with much greater suspicion and cynicism by the news editors. However, the same type of policy-free events took place and Central Office were getting up to four photo-opportunities in each early evening news, although the reporters' voice-overs increasingly pointed out how contrived these events were. By 1987 all three parties were energetically pursuing coverage using Reece's concept, but the media now, rather wearily, were covering the 'photo-ops' simply because they could not afford to miss one that might turn out to be real news.

The most important result of the photo-opportunity was to increase the focus on the personalities of the leaders. ITN invented the idea of 'target teams' who were dedicated completely to following the party leaders everywhere they went. The other important consequence was that the reporter on the team was often forced into providing instant commentaries on the pictures (in order to beat the ever-increasing competition to air), and so mature reflection on events was not possible, only snap judgements. This in turn increasingly led the editors to hire specialists from the writing press who could be relied upon to handle this greater responsibility without close editorial supervision.

It is quite clear that both ITN and BBC radically changed their policy regarding photo-opportunities after the 1987 election. Stewart Purvis (ITN's editor in chief) took the line that in future these events were to be treated solely on a 'new value' basis, while Tony Hall (director of BBC News and Current Affairs) went further. 'Photo-opportunites', he said, 'are of little worth unless they go wrong, and for the most part I wouldn't bother to use them'.

News editors are only now challenging the theoretical basis of Gordon Reece's concept that, because the event exists it is news. As Michael Brunson of ITN says, 'If a minister thinks that just by going out and having himself photographed in a hospital we are suddenly going to feature the government's record on NHS spending, he needs his head read.'

The media continue to fall for some image-making scams, however, like the current 'grand advertising poster unveiling' scam, which involves buying a few poster sites around London and briefing the BBC and ITN that this is the start of a 'massive' national poster campaign.

The cameras duly turn up and naïvely film a politician drawing back the covers on the poster, which of course is now worth a fortune, having gathered priceless exposure on prime-time news. The 'massive' campaign is then quietly abandoned.

Both Purvis and Hall believe that in future there will be more analysis of the issues, less reliance on the visual and increased focus on the verbal. Unless the party professionals devise events that exemplify their policies, they risk losing coverage. Up to now broadcasters (largely for self-protection) have equated 'balance' with time given to each party. This 'stop-watch' balance is fast disappearing (to the detriment of third parties) as news programmes take over from newspapers as the main source of historical record (after all, who would prefer to read a speech of Disraeli's rather than watching it on video?).

Photo-opportunities are being gradually reduced to convent-ient 'underlay' footage as part of a larger plan by broadcasters to educate rather than entertain. Not only have the media stopped being the willing co-conspirators of the image makers but, as the image makers' profile grows, the cameras are increasingly being turned on them in an attempt to 'review' their work.

The lesson for the image makers in business, politics or the pressure groups, is to return to the low profile they enjoyed before 1979 and devise events that visualize the benefits of policy, rather than ever more desperate attempts to catch the voters' eye. They could do worse than follow the example of the royal family's image makers, who are extremely adept at getting coverage for various causes and charities supported by the Princess of Wales, by arranging suitable photo-opportunities. The Palace have cleverly managed to increase media access without engaging in the kind of stunts and gimmicks that politicians have engaged in.

Remember that the first ever walkabout was not by a politician, but instead took place in New Zealand in 1969 on a royal visit. The technique was immediately copied by the Labour party in the 1970 election on the suggestion of Wilson's political adviser, Marcia Williams (later Lady Falkender).

## Interviews

The second method of ensuring the 'right' kind of media coverage is the management of interviews, which are events with more potential for error than any other (bar perhaps news conferences). Interviews are not about the search for knowledge, they are about performance. And as Bernard Ingham said, 'Good PR is nine tenths anticipation and one tenth execution.'

Interviewers are trying hard to get noticed by bosses and peers and will be trying even harder to avoid making a mistake. The interviewee is often doing the same. Interviewers are usually trying to hide their ignorance: interviewees are trying even harder to hide the truth. The latter isn't that hard, given that a cabinet minister, say, or a chief executive, has usually been doing that job a lot longer than the journalist and knows a lot more about the subject than even the specialist reporter. The average television or radio interviewer is often too busy thinking about their next question or how to edit the piece than the actual answers they are getting. So what is the danger for the principal? In short, nerves, inexperience, lack of preparation, non-verbal leakage and a nasty tendency people have to tell the truth. It is the news manager's job to prevent all of these things getting out of hand – which is why the good ones are none too popular with interviewers.

There are eight basic types of interview: newspaper 'transcript'; newspaper 'profile'; news 'bite' (doorstep, down the line and pre-record); extended; documentary (either 'salami' or studio); phone-in, news conference; and debate.

## Newspaper transcripts

Newspaper transcript interviews (where questions are submitted in writing and written replies are supplied) are now rare events but are still sometimes used if the paper is completely hostile or particularly distrusted, eg the *Daily Mirror* interviewing Mrs Thatcher. Although, despite the fact that 18 per cent of *Mirror* readers vote Conservative, the paper's suggestion was invariably turned down even on this basis.

## Newspaper 'profiles'

Much more common are newspaper 'profile' interviews. Ever since the days of the American interviewer, Rex Reed, this type of interview has been practised by graduates from the Tomas de Torquemada school of interviewing, who have made their name (and fortune) being spectacularly hostile to the interviewee. The problem here is that the interviewer is quite convinced they are the real star of the show – and not the interviewee. It is absolutely vital that no principal should *ever* be under any doubt that their motivation is to write a critical piece. They are not interested in the interviewee's achievements, but rather in scandal, gossip, sexual peccadillo, failing, weakness, eccentricity, physical disability or vulnerability. They cannot be charmed, diverted, flattered or seduced – that, after all, is *their* stock in trade and one at which they excel. Most agree with Louis Heren's advice to journalists interviewing politicians, which was to 'Keep asking oneself – why is this bastard lying to me?' It should be a strict rule that under no circumstances *whatsoever* should any principal agree to be interviewed by a journalist who has their name in the title eg *The Brenda Barker Interview*.

Not only should the profile interviewer be vetted very carefully (at the very least every interview they have conducted over the last few years should be analyzed) but their game plan also has to be accurately assessed. It is as important to predict what they want out of the interview, as it is for the interviewee (and their image makers) to decide what it is they want to say.

## TV manners

Television interviewers obviously cannot get away with being either as hypocritical or as judgemental as this, nor – as they are professional journalists (and not licensed bullies) – do they have any wish to.

In general, courtesy and politeness to journalists should be *de rigeur* (unless greatly provoked) before and during the interview, not least because the audience often views the interviewer as a friend of the family and gets very upset when they are patronized or insulted. For example, I remember vividly the time when a very senior politician (who had just been the victim of a classic stitch-up) was invited by David Dimbleby to appear on a discussion programme he was chairing. Dimbleby was silent as a red-faced politician stood only inches away, prodding him hard in the chest with his forefinger. 'I'll do your fucking [prod] programme,' he hissed at him, 'but I'll be fucking [prod] angry [prod] while I'm doing it.' He did and he was. The object should be to keep the conversation on an Adult–Adult basis – to use terms from transactional analysis. If, for example, the interviewer asks, 'Why is the government not spending more to clear this problem up?' and the interviewee answers 'Why are you always criticizing and blaming us for the ills of society?' he is acting as a child would.

There are even opportunities during interviews for building Parent–Child relationships, eg when Peter Lilley destroyed Francine Stock in a recent interview on *Newsnight* he did so in the classic manner of a parent irritated with a teenager's naïveté and woolly thinking. The dangers of being patronizing are obvious, but it can be very effective to exploit the interviewee's principal advantage, ie he or she knows more about the subject than the interviewer.

The worst scenarios of all are evidently Child–Child interviews, those which have degenerated into slanging matches based on the traditional pantomime dialectic of the 'Oh yes you did', 'Oh no I didn't' variety. This is a particular danger when the two people concerned are not in the same room and can't see each other. The Radio 4 *Today* radio car is a favourite venue.

## On the doorstep

Owing to the pace of newsgathering, the growth in ENG and the viewers' ever-decreasing attention span, 'doorstep' news interviews are now very common, so called because they often take place as the interviewee exits from meetings, eg trade union and employers' negotiations. A novel and very effective variation of the 'doorstep' was practised by Sir Michael Edwardes during the British Leyland dispute in 1979. Reporters were briefed on the time he would leave his office by car, Edwardes would wind down his window, deliver a 'bite', wind the window up again and drive off.

They are very useful ways of getting across a very brief message or 'bite', yet without very careful handling they can turn into either an unsightly scrum of jostling reporters or an opportunity for reporters to ask follow-up questions. The Reagan White House adopted the method of allowing press corps pool journalists to shout out questions as the president crossed the White House lawn on his way to his helicopter. If any question was to his liking he answered it cheerfully and went on his way. If he didn't like the question, he simply cupped his hand to his deaf ear, shrugged as if to say he didn't quite catch the question, waved cheerily and disappeared. Mrs Thatcher used the same technique (entering her car outside No 10) during the ill-fated second ballot of the leadership contest, to give out (at Bernard Ingham's suggestion) the simple message, 'I fight on, I fight to win'. John Major takes the opportunity to study prompt cards in the small hall next to the front door of No 10 before going out to answer questions from the reporters in their pen outside the Foreign Office.

The rules for a successful doorstep are first, the cameras must not obstruct the principal's path; secondly, they must be stationary some yards away; thirdly, some physical means, eg crush barriers, needs to be employed to restrain the camera crews; fourthly, minders have to be present to brief the crews on the timing of the interviewee's appearance (as video cameras need a few seconds to run at full speed); fifthly, the minders must scan the background 'in frame' (ie the area the cameras will include), to remove or conceal extraneous distractions or embarrassments; and lastly, the interviewee must briefly rehearse the 'bite' before leaving or entering the building.

The importance of preparation is illustrated in this story. On the taking of South Georgia, Bernard Ingham correctly predicted that, on hearing the news, reporters outside No 10 would ask: 'What next?'. Mrs Thatcher refused to believe they could be capable of this reaction and no answer was rehearsed. It turned out that Ingham was right, which is the origin of Mrs Thatcher's startled and irritated rejoinder: 'Just rejoice in that news.' (Usually misquoted as 'Rejoice! Rejoice!').

### Taking it down the line

I was always very reluctant to agree to 'down-the-line' interviews, where the interviewee is in a studio with a 'remote' (unmanned) camera, being questioned by an interviewer in a studio miles away – although logistically it was often difficult to arrange a face-to-face meeting. First, they are often 'live', with no room for mistakes and no facility for re-takes. Secondly, interviewers, emboldened by their situation, tend to be more aggressive and interrupt more often, and these interviews can degenerate into ill-tempered slanging matches. Thirdly, it places the interviewee in the uncomfortable position where they cannot see the interviewer (although they can be seen themselves), or gauge any reaction to what they have said. They rely totally on an ear-piece to hear the questions and these studios are often small, hot, and lack make-up facilities. Lastly, the interviewee is usually instructed by the studio manager to look directly into the lens, which is both disturbing for the viewer (see the 'super stare' in Chapter 2) and for the interviewee, who has only the blackness of the camera lens for company, often preventing them from relaxing into a friendly attitude.

If possible the interviewee should be looking not at the lens but just to one side. In fact, it is best of all if the interviewee should be looking at the minder. This allows them to explain their point to another human being who can react encouragingly. It also prevents any tendency some nervous interviewees have to give out the wrong visual signals, eg to any question that requires that the response should be in the negative, the aide simply shakes their head towards the end of the question. The interviewee will automatically follow that lead and start off their answer with a firm, confident 'No', and not a feeble 'Yes, but ...'.

### Pre-recorded 'bites'

News managers have long looked askance at news bites in the

form of pre-recorded interviews, because they fear that their principal's views will suffer in the editing process. I have always disagreed with this generalized view as – if handled correctly – they can be a very effective way of getting the bite to the viewer.

The interviewer's game plan usually consists of getting one or two answers of either a 'What is/has been going on?' or a 'What do you say in reply to ... ?' kind. If these coincide with the image maker's plans then the only task is to rehearse the bite properly to warm the principal up (very few interviewees do themselves justice at the first attempt) and to maintain the discipline of repeating the bite, whatever the question, in the interview itself.

For example, take this fairly typical (but fictionalized) exchange between politician (or it could be a business leader) and reporter.

*Q*: Minister, what is your reaction to the Jones Report condemning your policy on future developments?
*A*: I welcome the report and fully intend to study its conclusions carefully over the next few days and, where appropriate, act on them. (This takes 11 seconds to say. Much shorter answers encourage the editors to use two answers. A longer answer encourages editors to cut out part of the reply.)
*Q*: (with mounting incredulity) But Minister, the report utterly condemns your current policy, calling it disgraceful, deplorable and disastrous!
*A*: (calmly) I welcome the report and fully intend (etc) ...
*Q*: (sensing blood) Are you trying to tell the public that you agree with the report's conclusions?
*A*: (see above)
*Q*: (getting irritated) Surely Sir, this means that your policy has to be stopped?
*A*: (see above)
*Q*: (with some bitterness) Following comments made on your own role in this affair, don't you think you should resign?
*A*: (see above)
*Q*: (sarcastically) Thank you very much, Minister.
*A*: (sweetly) No, thank *you* very much.

The news that evening will inevitably consist of a reporter standing on a windswept College Green opposite the Houses of Parliament saying 'the government today denied opposition claims that the Jones Report was an indictment on its record'. Cut to Minister, 'I welcome ...'.

If the interviewer's game plan is to seek the answer to a question in an area that the principal does not want to touch upon, then the latter has to be relentless in bringing the discussion back to the bite. *In extremis*, one could always try Attlee's method of dealing with difficult questions. He would favour the unfortunate interviewer with a long, silent, stony look and then say brusquely: 'What's your next question?' If in this example the Jones Report is a subject to be avoided then the answer can be constructed to acknowledge its existence but divert attention away from it (or its conclusions), eg 'While I welcome the Jones Report, the important thing is that we stick to our successful policy of ...'. One recent research study identified 35 ways of not answering questions in interviews.

'Pre-records' give the principal both that vital opportunity to rehearse and a chance for retakes if the listening minder spots an error. Unlike live interviews, they are fairly predictable in that the content is usually known, even arranged, in advance. In a live interview, the reporter may well change the subject to one for which no line has been prepared, or even to an issue or event (especially in a fast-moving news story) of which the principal has no knowledge. To reduce the element of surprise the news manager needs to have first-class media monitoring back-up and must be in constant contact with it. What I used to do was this; when out of the office I used always to carry a 1-in television in my pocket. This allowed me to monitor news broadcasts through the day, wherever I was. My day began at 7.30 am in my office with a reading of all 12 daily papers (ie including the Communist *Morning Star*) from front to back. At weekends I had read the relevant sections of the Sunday papers by midnight on Saturday.

### Extended interviews – the importance of preparation

Extended interviews take much greater time to prepare and, given their enormous importance to the political process, this time should never be skimped. These interviews involve a five-stage process: assessing the bid; negotiating the conditions; briefing the principal; rehearsal; and post-interview appraisal.

Bids are assessed on the basis of upside/downside, timing, need to say, and which interviewer is being used. The first of these is easily the most important, as the risk of making errors or of giving oxygen to a story that is dying is always present. Bernard Ingham's rule was that no story lasts more than nine days if no new discoveries/ramifications appear. Hard questions have to be asked. Is there something new to say? Is this the time to say it? What is the benefit to the principal? Is it worth the time and effort needed to carry out a successful interview? Is the intent of the interviewer basically constructive? If these questions can't *all* be answered confidently and positively, then the bid should be declined.

If the bid is accepted, then the host's agenda should be discussed with their production team and conditions (place, time, interviewer, others appearing, studio set etc) have to be negotiated carefully. The question of the interviewer could be important. As one journalist once explained to me, (when I asked him where his self-confident air came from), he couldn't take seriously any of the cabinet ministers with whom he had been at university.

The principal then has to be briefed, initially in writing. This brief covers the questions that will be asked; the right answers; the interviewer's objective; what the principal should seek to get out of the interview. There should also be a background briefing on the programme (eg is there a preceding film?); names of others appearing on the programme; tapes of previous interviews; transcripts or minutes taken from the meetings between the news manager and the host's production team. This should be backed up with a verbal briefing so that the principal has a chance to ask any questions or voice any worries.

Then, the day before the interview, a full rehearsal must take place with the most senior manager acting as the interviewer. The principal is reminded that posture and breathing are important and the more obvious body language deficiencies (eg folding the arms defensively) are pointed out. A special point has to be made of the speed at which we talk when adrenalin is flowing freely. As anyone who has been interviewed live knows, the time goes by in a flash.

It is vital that the person playing the interviewer in the rehearsal has no fear of acting frankly, even unpleasantly and aggressively. A good rehearsal is designed not only to protect the principal from surprises or errors, but also to give them the confidence to face anything the opposition has to offer. If the rehearsal goes badly, then time must be allocated on the day itself to go through the process again.

The minder (together with a fact file containing all the information that may be discussed) then accompanies the principal to the studio; keeps them in a relaxed and confident mood; supervises the make-up; checks the studio setting on the monitors (eg making sure the seats are at the same height); and gives out last-minute reminders, warnings and advice on tactics.

As our saliva production ceases when we are anxious, a glass of water near to hand is a necessity. Our bodies react in other ways that can also cause problems: the heart pumps faster (to rush the blood from viscera to muscle and brain), so a reminder to pause before speaking is necessary. We sweat and the blood recedes from the skin, so more make-up may be needed.

A brief discussion may also be needed to remind the principal that, whatever the first question, it's often best to ignore it, and start by saying 'Before answering that I'd like to point out ...'. A quick word of encouragement or a joke to relax them before the floor manager's signal, then the red light above the camera winks on and we're off.

Here is an example of the preparation for an actual interview taken more or less at random from my diaries.

In November 1989 the political situation was as follows. The Tory party was well behind Labour in the polls and consequently party morale was suffering. There had been a series of inter-necine arguments concerning European policy and Mrs Thatcher had been portrayed as unreasonably anti-EC. There had been much speculation about Mrs Thatcher's future owing to statements she had made confirming she would not contest a fifth election and then saying she would 'go on and on'. There was also a bid for the Tory party leadership election in December by Sir Anthony Meyer.

Bernard Ingham had accepted a bid from the BBC's *Panorama* programme for Monday, 27 November, as part of the post-Queen's Speech prime ministerial programme of interviews. He had submitted, as usual, a written minute to Mrs Thatcher that weekend – what he used to call his 'stage directions and script' – covering the points outlined above, plus suggested demeanour and tone of voice. On the day of the interview the subject was discussed in the Week Ahead Meeting (WAM) at No 10 (see Bernard Ingham's account in *Killing the Messenger*, p 212) which, on this day, my diary records, started at 10 am. The first subject to be discussed was the question of the prime minister's future. After a short discussion it was suggested that she should say that she would go on 'as long as the electorate and the party want me to', and she agreed that this formula should put a stop to the endless speculation (which it did). Secondly, we touched on the difficulty of being behind in the polls. At the time I had a strict policy of not making any comment on poll ratings because firstly they are only a snapshot in time and secondly if you comment on one you are forced to keep commenting on each succeeding one.

We knew that David Dimbleby would be the interviewer and I was keen on putting him off his stride, as his strong point (like Frost) is a kind of insouciant self-confidence which sustains him during an interview. As to technique, he is fond of the 'past words and present contradictions' ploy, which consists of digging up words from old speeches, articles and interviews which conflict with the interviewee's current policies or ideas. A variant is the 'differences with colleagues' gambit, which is designed to demonstrate divisions among partners.

## The interviewers

We puzzled over the problem of Dimbleby that morning until we remembered that he had anchored the disastrous BBC 1987 *Election Night Special*, when he announced at the start of the programme that their exit poll predicted that the Conservatives' lead was only 5 per cent (the result was in fact an 11 per cent lead). So we agreed that, as soon as he mentioned polls, the prime minister would attack right back with something along the lines of 'Well, we all know how accurate the polls are, or have you forgotten the exit poll you announced in 1987?'

Later that morning I sent a videotape over to No 10 of Dimbleby's appearance on the programme. In the interview itself Mrs Thatcher pounced as planned. Dimbleby was only briefly shaken and recovered quickly, but he had lost the initiative and quickly moved on to another subject.

The longest part of the discussion was on Europe. I felt strongly at this time that she must be seen to be more positive in tone, because that would allow her to attack those EC measures like the Social Charter, that we opposed implacably, even more strongly – without being accused of being *wholly* negative. I suggested that she took the opportunity that the interview gave her of starting in a positive vein by outlining the virtues and benefits of the single market (which was the best example of her free market, '*union des patries*' vision of Europe). I had also been very keen over that summer that we make 'federalism' a dirty word (as the Republicans in America had made liberalism a dirty word in the 1988 election a year before), so it was agreed that she would attack the vision of a centralized superstate and use the f-word to characterize those who not only wanted to locate power in the centre, but wanted an interventionist bureaucracy to run this centre. Thus, a double whammy was agreed: first be positive about 1992; then launch an attack on federalism.

After tying up a few loose ends on other subjects and agreeing some defensive lines to take on more minor issues, the meeting ended at 11.30am. Later that day Ingham sat with the prime minister going over the main points yet again and then supervized the recording itself. The prime minister's performance was (as usual) nervous at first, but she warmed up well. All the questions we had anticipated were asked and she answered them exactly as agreed, fluently and forcefully, without straying too far from the agreed lines. Much of the preparation for interviews is a question of building up the interviewee's confidence, as it is fear of surprises that makes them nervous. The more predictable the experience, the less the anxiety will be. As the interview progresses the interviewee realizes that they are on top of the situation and then their self-confidence blossoms. Mrs Thatcher was once very nervous before appearing live on *Wogan*, but her anxiety completely disappeared when (to her amazement) she realized that he was reading all his questions off large 'idiot boards' placed just out of camera shot.

The prime minister herself rarely had time for post-interview appraisals (although she was an avid viewer of television news, she always refused to watch herself on television), relying instead on Bernard Ingham's verdict. Lesser mortals are, however, well advised to sit down afterwards and discuss frankly with their news managers and policy advisers how the performance could be improved next time. As we are particularly incapable of recognizing our own failures of body language, they especially need to be pointed out by others.

In an effort to gain the upper hand, minders routinely analyze the strengths and weaknesses of interviewers in this manner. For example, some interviewers have short fuses, so are easy to needle. They also lack self-discipline and interrupt incessantly, which can also be exploited profitably.

The world's expert at needling is Arthur Scargill, the miners' leader who developed a whole battery of techniques designed to provoke the interviewer into making statements that could then be turned against them. No wonder he once said he would have liked to have been a barrister.

Take this example of controlled aggression in a 1983 interview with Peter Snow on the BBC television *Newsnight* programme. Snow began by asking Scargill why he had not attacked Andropov's actions in Afghanistan.

*Scargill*: Have you read my full speech in Moscow?

*Snow*: Yes, I have.

*Scargill*: Have you? I don't believe you. I'm sorry. Have you seen the full text, honestly?

*Snow*: I have not seen any reference in that text to an attack on what President Andropov's troops are doing in Afghanistan or the military government in Poland.

*Scargill*: Have you seen the full text, because other broadcasters have told me they have not? Have you seen it, truthfully?

*Snow*: I have not seen any reference...

*Scargill*: I did not ask that. Have you seen the full text?

*Snow*: Would you answer my question? [Interruption] Well, I am asking the questions if I may say so.

*Scargill*: Oh no, not this time, you're not. I am asking you if you have seen the full text.

*Snow*: Well, to be quite honest, I have not seen the full text.

*Scargill*: Right, now I will answer your question, now you have admitted you have not seen the full text.

Brian Walden's weakness, conveniently for the interviewee, is that he likes to answer his own questions, so half the interview is taken up with him ruminating in a leisurely fashion. However, one has to be alert to his putting words into one's mouth. He does this by means of his notorious 'summaries', disguised as friendly attempts to 'clarify', using phrases like 'Let's just see if I understand you'.

Take this example of a lamb (William Waldegrave) being led by Walden to the slaughter and (to mix the metaphor thoroughly) making policy on the hoof:

*Waldegrave*: We do not intend to extend tax relief for private health care.

*Walden*: Are you going to get rid of the tax relief that exists?

*Waldegrave*: That is a matter for the chancellor and his budget. I have to say it hasn't worked very well. It's expensive to administer, and it hasn't really been taken up, I would gather, very widely.

*Walden*: Oh, this is a kind of double plus pledge. Not only, and now let's be clear that I am not misunderstanding you, not only is there no question of any further tax relief for private health for anybody of any age, but also you're very dubious about whether that that exists already has done any good, and we shouldn't drop dead with shock if it turns out that in the budget it's withdrawn.

*Waldegrave*: I think that would put it very fairly.

Monday's headlines (which was what Walden was after) shrieked 'Waldegrave hoist on health tax gaffe' and the treasury was forced to smack the minister down smartly. By the Wednesday of that week, Mr Waldegrave was back on television to confess the error of his ways.

It was my view while working in Central Office that Michael Brunson and James Naughtie were probably the least egotistical and most effective interviewers in broadcasting today, but one should always be careful to challenge their tendency to introduce doubtful premises, along the lines of 'many observers say ...' (ie Mrs Brunson said at breakfast) or 'informed sources claim ...' (ie a man Mr Naughtie met in the Duck & Dive claims). Sir Robin Day on the other hand thinks he is more important than the interviewee and can be led astray by flattery.

## Documentary interviews

All of the above also applies to an interview used as part of a documentary, if, that is, the interview is live and follows the film.

If it is pre-recorded and edited (like slices of salami) into the film, then the most important part of the process is discovering exactly what precedes and succeeds that portion of the interview, as it is the juxtaposition of images that can often do the most to distort meaning. Extra care must be taken to analyze the principal's answers carefully and insist on re-takes if the slightest error appears. These 'contracts' cannot normally be enforced by government or business minders but the Palace insists on written terms and conditions and a veto on the rough-cut. The Palace also controls the copyright on footage of royal events.

## The dreaded phone-in

When a news manager has nightmares they usually feature either as a phone-in interview, a news conference or a televised debate. It's not that phone-in interviews are different in technique from the live extended interview, but it is impossible for the principal to be even the least bit rude to a member of the public. If one replies to an ordinary citizen in a combative way that would be perfectly acceptable when talking to a professional interviewer, then all hell would break loose in the media. Moreover the citizen can be as rude as they like. For example, in the notorious 'Belgrano' 1983 election phone-in, Mrs Thatcher was asked why the Argentine ship was sunk while sailing away from the Falklands. Her obvious frustration at feeling herself unable to fight back against her persistent questioner was matched only by the latter's hectoring and unpleasant manner.

## News conferences

News conferences have a dreadful tendency to go wrong, mainly because it is impossible to control the media's agenda. They decide the news of the day and that's what they will ask questions on. If these coincide with the objective of the conference, then fine; but the point of the exercise is often lost.

The key to a successful news conference is preparation. Larry Speakes, in his memoirs, shows how sophisticated a process this is for the president of the United States. First, a date for the news conference was set two weeks in advance and all departments of state (and other government agencies) were asked what subjects

[169]

they thought would come up and to supply questions and answers for each issue. On the Friday before the Tuesday conference, Reagan would receive a briefing book containing all this information for him to study at Camp David. On Monday afternoon at 2 o'clock, the president's chief aides would gather in the family's cinema, which would be set up with presidential podium, TV lighting, microphone and a reporters' table where Speakes and his team would sit.

On the basis that journalists were just there to trap the president into admitting or exposing something he should not, Speakes tried in these rehearsals (which lasted two hours) to do the same. The whole process was then repeated for another two hours on Tuesday afternoon. This may seem a lot, but it should be compared with Nixon's practice of doing nothing else but rehearse for the entire 48-hour period before his news conferences.

Before going into the East Room, where the reporters were assembled, Reagan used to have a briefing session with Speakes who picked out reporters from a huge board representing the layout of the room. Each space on the board had a photo of the reporter, plus their name and organization. Speakes would then order the White House television producer to have his cameras scan the room and, while Reagan watched on the monitors, he would provide a running commentary on the assembled journalists. He would then brief the president on exactly where to call questions from. Those in the back row were not to be called as they were mavericks. Those on the right were those who traditionally asked friendly questions. After the meeting, Speakes would mount a spin patrol to assess the media's reaction and encourage a favourable appraisal. Speakes calculated that he usually anticipated 90 per cent of the questions. Nonetheless, even granted that Reagan was perhaps not the most adept of Presidents in this area, this experience underlined the point that news conferences are very difficult for news managers to regard as anything other than a disaster waiting to happen.

Of course, questions can be planted among friendly journalists; indeed, virtually all the questions asked at General de Gaulle's twice-yearly news conferences were plants. Pierre Salinger developed the successful technique of ringing reporters up the day before Kennedy's press conferences and telling them that if they were to ask a certain question next morning they were sure to receive 'an interesting answer'. I preferred the corollary technique of planting difficult questions in the audience of Labour party press conferences, often with very satisfactory results.

The fact is that, as a method of shaping the news, news conferences are only as good as the principal's ability to think clearly under pressure. Bernard Ingham convinced Mrs Thatcher that news conferences, far from being disasters waiting to happen, were opportunities to get her point across, but that was on the basis that he had complete faith in her intellectual abilities and quick wits. Lesser mortals often succumb to the pressure, and that's when mistakes can happen.

## Debates

The same problems attend the management of debates. Debates between leaders are now common in US politics (since Ford agreed to debate with Carter, every election has seen debates between the two main contenders) and there is heavy pressure by the broadcasters to repeat the experience in Britain. In my view any incumbent who accepts the challenge of their opponent in this form needs their head examined. The latter has very little to lose and the former very little to gain.

In 1976 Carter exploited Ford's mistake (Ford said that Eastern Bloc countries weren't under Soviet control); then Reagan, in 1980, destroyed Bush in the New Hampshire primary debate and went on to do the same to Carter with his famous put down 'there you go again'. The history of the last 30 years is littered with examples such as these.

## Which type of interview to choose?

A news manager's function is to keep on top of events and their methods are designed to give them the greatest amount of control over how events are perceived. As news conferences and debate-type interviews offer the least possibilities for control, it follows that they should only be considered if the alternatives are unavoidable. When they *are* mandatory or unavoidable, eg elections, post-summit, presidential etc, then the news manager's object should be to anticipate the questions, rehearse the answers, and encourage the principal – having said what they came to say – to leave immediately.

The best way to anticipate questions is to study the interests of paticular journalists carefully, in the same way that the prime minister's aides study the interests of MPs who have put down a parliamentary question. This process invariably pays dividends in predicting what the subject matter of their question will be.

## The wordsmiths

The greatest amount of control that a news manager can achieve over what is reported is when they are using speeches or articles to get the message across – which is why the wordsmiths have become so important. The briefers are also not above creating the odd *bon mot* for their masters; for example, Mrs Thatcher's verdict on Gorbachev ('A man we can do business with') was suggested by Sir Bernard Ingham. They are even sometimes fictionalized. Larry Speakes later admitted that his report after the Geneva summit that President Reagan had told Gorbachev that the 'world breathes easier because we are meeting' was untrue. Speakes simply felt that Reagan might have said it.

Ever since Corax of Syracuse wrote the first rhetoric manual and Aristotle stressed the need for politicians to learn the skills of public speaking in order to communicate their ideas persuasively, speeches have been a mainstay of political communications. Indeed one cannot better Aristotle's analysis (in *Rhetoric*) of the three keys to oratorical persuasion:

– illuminating the personal character of the speaker;
– putting the audience in the right frame of mind; and
– providing proof of thesis.

It is only 30 years since Harold Wilson was constantly reminding his audiences that his speeches were entirely his own work, unlike those of Sir Alec Douglas-Home. Home had hired a team of speechwriters (including Nigel Lawson from the *Sunday Telegraph*), because he was unfamiliar with social and economic issues and the use of speechwriters was designed to make up for these deficiencies. The news leaked and was used by Labour as yet more evidence that Home was not intellectually equipped to do the job. In fact Wilson, when in power, used Joe Haines (his press secretary), Antony Wedgwood Benn and Marcia Williams as his writing team and soon it became accepted by the media that speeches would be the work of hired hands.

Mrs Thatcher's first conference speech in 1975 was largely the work of (later Sir) Ronnie Millar and he continued to be an important contributor to every party conference speech that she made thereafter. He also helped draft John Major's first conference speech in 1991. It was Millar who came up with the most memorable image-making line since Gaitskell's 'Fight, fight and fight again', when he wrote her defiant challenge to the wets (paraphrasing Christopher Fry's play title) 'U-turn if you want to, the lady's not for turning'.

## Image-making humour

Millar and John O'Sullivan, the editor of the *National Review*, also performed a vital image-making task for Mrs Thatcher by making her speeches funny; vital because there are not that many opportunities to communicate a leader's sense of humour, outside of speeches.

Now that rallies are ticket only, even the chance to put down hecklers wittily has disappeared. Wilson's reputation for humour depended on sallies like (to a man who threw leaflets at him and missed) 'Your aim is as good as your material'. When a pro-Rhodesian asked him 'Why are you talking to savages?', Wilson snapped back, 'We don't talk to savages, we just let them come to our meetings'.

Mrs Thatcher's own sense of humour was not obviously 'jokey', which is generally the style the British like best. The nearest I can get to a description is 'wry' or perhaps 'mis-chievous'. Let me take one example from my diary. One morning, at the start of our regular Monday meeting, the Prime Minister suddenly asked, to our surprise, if any of us knew anything about wild flowers. After a moment's silence, Peter Morrison, the Deputy-Chairman of the Party, said somewhat diffidently that he 'knew a bit'. The Prime Minister then asked 'How big is the flower, the scarlet pimpernel?' Peter said 'I'm afraid I don't know, Prime Minister. Why do you want to know?' She replied 'Because tomorrow morning I'm off to Paris to attend the bicentenary celebrations of the French Revolution, and I thought I would wear one in my button-hole'.

Millar was extremely adept at catching this slightly sly, tongue-in-cheek style and, although the commentators continued to charge Mrs Thatcher with the un-British crime of not having a sense of humour, excerpts from her speeches on the television annually contradicted them.

Ronald Reagan, by contrast, was a naturally funny man who could ad lib jokes better than any recent US president since Roosevelt. For example, semi-conscious on a trolley after being shot by John Hinckley, Reagan looked up at the nurse holding his hand comfortingly and asked, 'Does Nancy know about us?'. Reagan was expert at a technique he developed when he was a sports announcer in Davenport, Illinois. Reagan had a group of friends in Des Moines who listened to his baseball commentaries at the local barber shop and he developed the habit of imagining them sitting around listening. He would then imagine how his words were sounding and how they might be reacting to them. He used the language, expressions and slang that he would have used if he had been in the shop describing the game to them face to face. From this experience he developed various dicta like always using short sentences and words of few syllables, or giving examples of what he meant to illustrate a point, and he made it a point to tell a joke or a funny story at the start of a speech in order to get people's attention. He was also a great believer in that most traditional oratorical format of 'Tell them what you are going to tell them, tell them, and then tell them what you've just told them'.

## A lack of gravitas?

What Reagan lacked, however, was *gravitas* and that is exactly what his principal wordsmith, Peggy Noonan, knew how to supply. A key attribute of an effective speechwriter is to have a good ear for the cadences and rhythms of the principal's speech patterns. Unlike many speechwriters, Noonan wrote speeches to be spoken and not read, and she was an expert at providing the president with words he found easy and natural to say. She also faithfully reproduced his characteristically optimistic and positive approach. 'I'll never forget' was always rendered as 'I'll always remember', and 'I am worried' became 'I am concerned'. She knew that the public Reagan was always acting, but she also knew that he was only acting the part of Ronald Reagan, President, so she could easily tailor the script to the part. Noonan was a member of the television generation (born in 1950), so she knew that modern audiences are now so used to commercials breaking up programmes that they aren't capable of concentrating for very long. With that in mind, she designed Reagan's speeches to have sections containing two or three minutes of 'good stuff', followed by the 'boring, obvious stuff' that allowed the audience to daydream.

Above all, Noonan provided the poetry. She wrote the extraordinarily moving speech that Reagan delivered at Pointe du Hoc on the 40th anniversary of D-Day and the unbearably poignant eulogy for the crew of the Challenger shuttle. 'We will never forget them,' she wrote, 'nor the last time we saw them, this morning, as they prepared for their journey and waved goodbye, and slipped the surly bonds of earth to touch the Face of God' (based on lines from '*High Flight*' by John Gillespie Magee Jnr).

Later, when Bush was seeking the presidency, she did the same for him. The speech she wrote for him at the nominating convention in New Orleans is worthy of Dos Passos. Noonan provided Bush with a philosophic model of the US: 'This is America:' Noonan wrote, 'the Knights of Columbus, the Grange, Hadassah, the Disabled American Veterans, the Order of Alepa, the Business and Professional Women of America, the Union Hall, the Bible study group, LULAC, Holy Name – a brilliant diversity spread like stars, like a thousand points of light in a broad and peaceful sky.'

In her memoirs Noonan also emphasized how important language and labels are in politics. In the Edwardian era, 'progressive' was the label everyone wanted to claim, while no one wanted to be a 'whig'. Then there were 'protectionists' and 'free traders', 'appeasers' and 'warmongers', 'internationalists' and 'isolationists', while in the early 1980s it was 'drys' versus 'wets' and later 'radicals' against 'consolidators'. Now 'federalists' fight 'Eurosceptics', but the object is always the same, to invent a vocabulary that will undermine the enemies' case.

[175]

Language is often a key determinant in winning the battle of ideas. For example, the Labour party successfully changed 'community charge' to 'poll tax' and 'self-governing' to 'opt out'; causing considerable damage to the Tory party's chances of electoral victory.

Demons are conjured up in this way so that the exorcists may arrive like the cavalry in the nick of time. 'Missing the bus', whether in the context of imperial expansion or European integration is held unquestioningly as a bad idea. Likewise, being 'out of step' or 'isolated' is unthinkingly viewed with terror.

Sociologists have introduced their own distorted vocabulary to politics; for example, when joy-riders riot in Newcastle, the Archbishop of Canterbury justifies their actions on the basis that they live in 'deprived' areas, yet no one ever explains what these people were deprived of, or who deprived them of it; it is simply taken for granted that it is true. Politicians confuse the voter with their talk of, for example, 'unilateralism' rather than 'one-sided'.

One of the most important contributions the image makers have made is to teach politicians and business leaders to drop all this silliness and to use the language of their real audience, the average customer and the ordinary voter, the simple, everyday language of the factory, office, shop and pub. They have warned of the dangers of jargon, Latinate words, unnecessary verbiage, and they have championed simplicity and clarity. In doing this they have made politics and business more interesting and relevant to the everyday lives of the British public, a contribution that cannot but have helped democracy flourish.

# Epilogue

*An idea is not responsible for its consequences*

Mark Twain

*All silencing of discussion is an assumption of infallibility*

John Stuart Mill

*It is seldom that liberty of any kind is lost all at once*

David Hume

When the first political party of note to be founded in modern times was launched in 1981, no one thought it strange that its name, slogan, logo, corporate colours or advertising should be designed by professional image makers like my old boss, Winston Fletcher. Positioning (the politician's only contribution) turned out to be the SDP's Achilles' heel. They came up with one which, loosely translated, read: 'a party that's not like the other two'. No one ever discovered what it *was* like.

The SDP's launch news conference was held in the Connaught Rooms before 500 journalists and obtained the equivalent of £20 million in free publicity. It was launched just as any other new product would be and, like most new products, it failed. As in business, so in politics, it is simply not possible to sell a product that the public does not need or want (at least, not twice).

History is littered with failures of image making, yet it continues to attract a great deal of critical comment, much of which seems to be based on the premiss that it is some kind of infallible ju-ju. The Left charge that policy is now being created by the image makers without thought for principle or ideology. The liberal chattering classes claim that the trivial is being elevated in importance over the substantial, and the fraudulent over the truthful. Some worry that today's leaders are no more than hollow men, stuffed only with the straw of presentation, while others are uneasy that American business methods are intruding into the quasi-sacred relationship between the people and their leaders.

The Left's view that image makers are now driving policy is only partially true. Certainly they were correct when they said that Peter Mandelson was influential in the Labour party's policy review process. In reply to my question on this subject, he confirmed Labour left-wingers' worst fears when he admitted that 'I had a hand in the changes'. The same could not, however, be said of the Tory party – at least, not under Margaret Thatcher's leadership. Take, for example, the poll tax. Both Sir Tim Bell and Sir Gordon Reece made numerous attempts in the spring of 1990 to persuade Mrs Thatcher to modify the tax – culminating in a lively discussion over dinner at Chequers in May 1990, when they failed to persuade her to increase VAT to pay for a massive drop in the level of the charge. She refused them on principle, while accepting that it might be a popular change. Her view was consistently that image advisers should stick to their last and not interfere in policy matters. In my experience, this is a view invariably shared by those leaders with strongly-held beliefs.

The Left do have a point, however, when they say that market research is now playing a bigger role in creating policy than ever before. Walter Lippman once wrote that 'statesmanship ... consists in giving the people not what they want, but what they will learn to want'. Statesmen like that hardly exist now. Politicians do not usually give the people what research says they want (eg capital punishment, an end to coloured immigration and the withdrawal of troops from Ulster), but they do increasingly turn to their research advisers to divine the best strategy of persuading others that they should want what is on offer.

For example, speeches are now routinely researched using the 'people meter' method. A suitable cross-section of the electorate is gathered to watch a video of a speech. Each person is equipped with a hand-held 'trigger', which records their reactions to the speaker, usually in terms of approval or disapproval. The results are tabulated and those sections of the speech that go down badly are jettisoned; those that are popular are kept and repeated.

More significantly, perhaps, political parties are increasingly using research to pick leading candidates for office and to select policy priorities. It is still comparatively rare for a policy to be created by research (the sale of council houses is a notable exception), but over the next half century the power of research to determine party platforms will wax and, as a consequence, the parties will inevitably move towards each other's position on the main issues, as the influence of ideology wanes.

The accusations, from what are laughably called the intelligentsia, that image making is a conspiracy of the shallow and fraudulent to fool the people by artifice, are in my view based on a particularly rancid form of intellectual snobbery. So certain are the chattering classes of the electorate's gullibility and feebleness of intellect that they insist on protecting them from such devilish practices. In fact, the people's common sense and unerring ability to spot a wrong 'un at a thousand yards is all the protection they really need. No human being is capable of sustaining an illusory personality for long, certainly not under television's beady eye. Image makers may be able to alter physical appearance and modify body language, but they can't create what really matters – strength of character and inner conviction.

It is true that any actor can fake sincerity, and most politicians are reasonably talented actors. The voter, however, has a shrewd and practised eye for fakery. Their 'betters' may be convinced that Lincoln's dictum does not apply to the uneducated masses (all of whom they believe can be fooled all of the time), but the masses themselves know better. It never occurs to these idiot savants that the poor, dear, innocent people might actually want a decent, genial, average Joe like Reagan to lead them, or that they might welcome repeatedly being struck on the head by a handbag full of convictions. They react on these occasions in the same way judges do when – despite careful guidance – a jury finds the defendant innocent: pained surprise. The fact is, they don't really approve of undiluted democracy. In their view the people are incorrigibly addicted to various politically incorrect practices and aren't really qualified to make considered choices about their own future. Image making is one on a long list of undesirable activities the thought police have constructed, like smoking, watching soap operas, reading tabloid newspapers, eating fried food and gambling – from whose ill-effects the working class are supposed to need protection. In reality, what the working class need protection from is anyone who thinks that their education, rank, religious beliefs or wealth entitles them to any deference due to their opinions.

Politicians don't lie because their image makers tell them to; they lie because they are human. Their lies come in the form of exaggeration, calculated omission and synthetic emotion – none of which is as wicked or damaging to the people's welfare as incompetence, laziness or wilful refusal to face facts. They mostly use artifice like actors do, to create the illusion of reality, not to deceive.

No one in real life is as clean, tidy and well groomed as they are because there is no need to be. The average voter does not have to appear on television daily – an entertainment medium devised to sell goods, where performance counts more than content. They do not have photographers pursuing them with telephoto, wide-angle and close-up lenses. They do not ever have to be prepared with a snappy sound-bite, for no one is very interested in their views on current events. They do not have to live in dread that some antisocial peccadillo or self-indulgent weakness of theirs will be revealed, as no one is very interested in their private lives. They do not normally experience the viciousness and disloyalty of colleagues that most politicians take for granted. In short, their failings and inadequacies are kept decently private, while those who aspire to lead us are subject to the merciless exposure of the righteous led by the media, who are increasingly given to feeding frenzy as their preferred *modus operandum*. What little protection artifice can provide – which isn't much – is fully justified, if only on the grounds of self-defence.

Those who would restrict the use of marketing techniques like advertising in the democratic process are part of an ever-growing movement which considers that free speech and a free press are no more than Utopian ideals not to be taken too

[180]

literally (a view none of the newly free peoples of Eastern Europe would endorse). If the claims made in political advertising are misleading, then it is the media's duty to point that out. Democracy will not be enhanced by restrictions on free speech, any more than the arguments against smoking are enhanced by misguided attempts to prohibit the advertising of tobacco.

The one criticism of political marketing that has some substance to it is the claim that democracy can be suborned by those leaders and interest groups with the largest budgets. While there are many case histories of large sums being expended on failed .campaigns, it is certainly true that smaller parties sometimes struggle to make their voice heard. It is certainly worth considering placing a limit on spending and a prohibition on any organisation, institution or foreign national from donating funds to political parties. If the latter wish to help persuade the electorate to vote for a particular cause, then they are at liberty to pay for their own advertising. The individual's right to dispose of their fortune in whatever fashion they think fit must, though, be considered inviolate.

There is also some merit in the arguments of those who (like Michael Shea in his book *Leadership Rules*) claim that image making has played an important part in ensuring that some 'empty suits' have gained power at the expense of those with genuine talent and vision. It is indeed true that mediocre leaders have been elevated to high rank by careful presentation, but they rarely survive exposure at altitude. When Daniel Boorstin wrote 'two centuries ago, when a great man appeared, people looked for God's purpose in him – today we look for his press agents', he overestimated the power of the image makers. Great leaders are not created by others, they create themselves.

# Selected Bibliography

Atkinson, Max *Our Masters' Voices*. Methuen, London, 1984.

Bernays, Edward L *Crystallizing Public Opinion*. Boni & Liveright, New York, 1923.

Blumler, Jay G and McQuail, Denis *Television in Politics*. Faber and Faber, London, 1968.

Boorstin, Daniel J *The Image*. Atheneum, New York, 1962.

Butler, David *et al The British General Election*. Macmillan, London, 1960–1988.

Cockerell, Michael *Live from Number 10*. Faber & Faber, London, 1988.

Ebermayer, E and Meissner, Hans-Otto trans Hagen, Louis *Evil Genius*. Allan Wingate, London, 1953.

Greenfield, Jeff *Playing to Win*. Simon & Schuster, New York, 1980.

Halberstam, David *The Powers That Be*. Dell, New York, 1979.

Hall Jamieson, Kathleen *Packaging The Presidency*. OUP, New York, 1984.

Heren, Louis *The Power of the Press*. Orbis, London, 1985.

Ingham, Bernard *Kill The Messenger*. Harper Collins, London, 1991.

Jones, Nicholas *Strikes and the Media*. Basil Blackwell, Oxford, 1986.

Keay, Douglas *Royal Pursuit – The Palace, The Press and The People*. Severn House, London, 1983.

L'Etang, Hugh *The Pathology of Leadership*. Heinemann, London, 1969.

McGinniss, Joe *The Selling of the President*. André Deutsch, London, 1970.

Machiavelli, Niccoló *The Prince*. Penguin, London, 1961.

McLuhan, Marshall *Understanding Media*. Routledge and Kegan Paul, London, 1964.

Margach, James *The Anatomy of Power*. W H Allen, London, 1979.

Mayer, Martin *Whatever Happened to Madison Avenue*. Little, Brown & Company, Boston, 1991.

Morris, Desmond *Manwatching*. Jonathan Cape, London, 1977.

Noonan, Peggy *What I Saw at the Revolution*. Random House, New York, 1990.

Olins, Wally *Corporate Identity*. Thames & Hudson, London, 1989.

Riesman, David *The Lonely Crowd*. Yale University Press, New Haven, 1952.

Salinger, Pierre *With Kennedy*. Cape, London, 1967.

Shea, Michael *Leadership Rules*. Century, London, 1990.

Speakes, Larry *Speaking Out*. Charles Scribner, New York, 1988.

Tunstall, Jeremy *The Media in Britain*. Constable, London, 1983.

Wallas, Graham *Human Nature in Politics*. Constable, London, 1910.

Ward, Ken *Mass Communications and the Modern World*. Macmillan, London, 1989.

White, Theodore H *America in Search of Itself*. Jonathan Cape, London, 1983.

# Index

ABC (American
Broadcasting Company)
136
accents 61-2
accountability 86
ad libs 74, 174
addresses 115
adultery 22
advertising 24, 42, 87, 145
police 96-7
strict restrictions 105
threat to introduce, to
BBC 151
Vatican 96
*see also* political
advertising
advertising agencies 28-9,
88, 100-1, 116, 124-5,
130
hired by Conservatives
30, 97, 102, 113
hired by Labour 111-12
affectation 61-2
ageism 48
Ailes, Roger 89, 103-4
Aims of Industry 106
Alexander technique 59
alienation effect 132
amplifiers 25
Andrew, Prince 66
Andropov, Yuri 167
animals, *see* pets
*Answers* (magazine) 15
appearance, *see* physical
appearance
applause manipulation 25
'appropriateness' 57
Aristotle 172
Armstrong, Lord 47
articulation 59, 60-1
artifice 182
Ashdown, Paddy 52
Associated Press 12
AT & T 68
atheism 68, 149
*Athenia* 26

attack campaigns 99-108,
111
Attlee, Clement (Earl
Attlee) 30, 132, 162
Atwater, Lee 89, 102, 104
audiences 173
'confiding' in 61
involvement/participation
117, 131, 132
manipulation 118;
applause manipulation
25
modern 175
real 176
Australian Labour party
115
authority 57, 58, 59
Avis 94, 100

BA (British Airways) 93, 94,
148
backbenchers 140, 147, 148
background 41, 62-80, 95,
132
Bagehot, Walter 36
Baird, John Logie 29
Baker, James 104
Baker, Kenneth 120, 121,
137
on 'image' 78
spin doctoring 139, 140,
141
Baldwin, Stanley 15, 72,
129, 130
*Baltimore Republican* 63
Barnum, P T 21
Barthes, Roland 107
Basham, Brian 145
BAT (British-American
Tobacco Co) 145, 146
BBC (British Broadcasting
Corporation) 29-30,
93-4, 118, 139-40, 149,
150, 169
Churchill's efforts to
commandeer 18

*Election Night Special*
(1987) 165
ministerial broadcasts 150
*Newsnight* 158, 167
*Nine O'Clock News* 72
*Panorama* 141, 158, 164
policy regarding photo-
opportunities 154-5
Radio 4 *Today* radio car
158
*Royal Family* film 35-7
*Tonight* 98
*24 Hours* 151-2
BCal 148
beards 46, 94
Beatles 71, 93
Beaverbrook, Lord 15, 129,
130
Behrens, Peter 119
*Belgrano* 169
Bell, Tim Sir 90, 106, 138,
143, 144, 145, 180
'benefits' of legislation 87-8
Benn, Anthony Wedgwood
98, 151, 173
Bentsen, Lloyd 90
Bernays, Edward L 17, 128,
143
Bernbach, Bill 100, 120
Bernstein, Leonard 71
bias 146, 149, 150
Bio-pics 22, 85, 111
Bird, Drayton 114, 116
Birdwell, Russell 21
birthplace 62-3
Bishop, Sir Michael 144
Black Friday panic (1869)
16
black role models 123
blackmail 145
blackshirts 129
blasphemy 68
body language 43, 49, 132,
167, 181
defensive 111, 163
*bon mots* 172

Boorstin, Daniel 152, 183
Bow, Clara 21
Bradford 138, 139
brands
  associations 122-4
  globalization 78
  image 144
  Number Two 29, 88-90
  personality 94-5
  positioning 86-97, 122
Branson, Richard 52, 66
breathing 58-9, 163
Brecht, Bertolt 132
Breslin, Jimmy 157
brewers 148
bribery 22
briefers 133-41, 143, 159,
  162, 172
Brinkley, David 31
British Gas 124
British Leyland 159
British Medical Association
  106
British Midland 144
British Shops and Stores
  Association 55
British Telecom 121
broadcasts 17-19, 25, 27,
  150-2
  Christmas, first 36
  'Daisy' 101, 102
  news 130, 162
  outside 29, 35, 153
  Party election 30, 98, 102
  *see also* radio; television
Brown, George 142
Brunel, Isambard Kingdom
  122
Brunson, Michael 140, 141,
  155, 168, 169
Bruschal 10
Bryan, William Jennings 17
'buggins' turn' 96
Bush, Barbara 71
Bush, George 48, 64, 72-3,
  89, 90, 92, 171
  campaign (1988) 102-4
  dress 54
  health scares 48
  Navy flier image 66
  nominating convention
    speech 175-6
Bush, Neal 70
Butler, D 97
Butler, R A 63, 142
by-elections 82


Cagney, James (Jimmy) 23,
  24
Callaghan, James, Lord 30,
  65, 90, 102, 112, 142
  appointment of family
    member 70
  popularity 75
cameras

closed-circuit 117, 118
ENG (electronic news
  gathering) 154, 159
outside broadcast 35
Campbell, Alastair 111
Canterbury, Archbishop of
  146, 176
Capone, Alphonse 22
Capra, Frank 22
Carnegie, Andrew 16
Carson, Johnny 47
Carter, Amy 71, 106
Carter, Billy 70
Carter, James Earl (Jimmy)
  48, 63, 77, 85, 90, 136,
  171
  showbiz endorsement 123
  use of family for electoral
    reasons 71, 105-6
Carter, Rosalynn 71
Casals, Pablo 71
Castle, Barbara 112
Catholics 66, 67, 68, 149
Cawston, Richard 35
CBS (Columbia
  Broadcasting System)
  19, 31, 32, 136
celebrities 22, 123-4
Challenger shuttle 175
challenger strategy 89, 90,
  92
Chamberlain, Neville 29, 72
Chanel, Coco 44
character 74, 85, 95, 181
Chase, Chevy 47
Chataway, Christopher 98
chattering classes 178, 179
Cheney, Dick 68
*Chicago Tribune* 19
Churchill, Randolph 71
Churchill, Sir Winston 26,
  31, 35, 65, 149
  courage 80
  disdain for television 30
  efforts to commandeer
    BBC 18
  health 45-7
  income from writing 69
  props 52
Cicero 100
cinema 19-27, 132
  *see also* films
civil rights 99
civil servants 147, 176
class 45, 57, 63-5, 78-9
  division by 62
  governing 70
  moneyed 52, 58
  working 54, 64, 153, 182
classlessness 64, 97
closed-circuit cameras 117,
  118
clothes 51-2, 56, 132
  'alibi' 54
  casual 32, 54

dressing to impress 52-6
Coca Cola 121, 124
Cockerell, Michael 109
Cole, Nat King 123
Collins, Norman 30, 98
colours 58, 59, 121
Colville, Commander 35
comic strips 24
common touch 63, 76-7
Commons, House of 13, 14,
  18, 30, 70, 151
  dressing for 53
communications 107, 131
  inventions increasing
    speed and ease of 16
  mass 10
  newspapers' hegemony
    over 17
  television as primary
    means of 34
  *see also* political
    communication
communism 24, 80
community charge, *see* poll
  tax
'competence and caring'
  strategy 92
computers 115-16
conferences
  news 130, 170-1, 172
  party 111, 116-18, 132,
    137
confidence 58, 74
Connally, John 136
Connery, Sean 123
Conservative Central Office
  14, 30, 80, 108, 116,
  138-40
  leaking from 143
  photo-opportunities 153,
    154
  refusal to release official
    portrait of Major 48
Conservative party 99, 106,
  115, 121, 129, 176
  advertising agencies hired
    by 30, 97, 102, 113
  leadership election bid
    (1989) 165
  morale (1989) 164
  1922 Committee 140, 141
  *see also* Disraeli; Eden;
    Heath; Home;
    Macmillan;
    Major; Thatcher
contextual manipulation 49
controlled aggression 167
conviction 73, 76, 78, 181
Coolidge, Calvin 18
Cooper, Courtney Ryley 23
Copland, Aaron 71
corporate colours 177
corporate identity
  programmes 119
cosmetic surgery 44-5, 57

Coutts & Co 94
Crawford, Cynthia 57
credibility 58, 95, 102, 134, 146
  of promises 42, 114
creed and colour 66-8
criminals 46, 66
Crippen, Dr H H 17
Cripps, Sir Stafford 142
crisis managers 128, 144-5
Cromwell, Thomas 10
cronies 71
Cronkite, Walter 130
Crosland, A 110
Crossman, Richard 142
Cunningham, Dr Jack 139
Custer, General G A 45
customer service 94

Dailey, Peter 131
*Daily Express* 129, 149
*Daily Mail* 15, 129, 149
*Daily Mirror* 15, 111, 149, 157
*Daily Telegraph* 12
Daley, Mayor 34
Daly, Barbara 48
databases 115, 116
Davies, Philippa 59, 60
Davis Jnr, Sammy 123
Day, Barry 109
Day, Sir Robin 150, 168
debates 171
Delane, J T 12, 142
Delaney, Barry 105
Delors, Jacques 120
demotic usage 62
dentistry 44-5
design 118-19
  architectural 119
  corporate identity programmes 119
  political 120-2
Dewe, Roddy 145
dictatorship 25
Dietrich, Marlene 20, 24
Dimbleby, David 151, 158, 165
diplomatic service 96
direct marketing 83, 114-16
dirty pictures 101-2
dirty tricks 103
Disney image 95
Disraeli, Benjamin 22, 67, 155
divorce 66
*Dixon of Dock Green* 97
documentary interviews 168-9
Dole, Elizabeth 136
Dole, Robert 136, 137
donating funds 183
Donovan, Terry 48, 109
'doorstep' news interviews 158-60

'down-the-line' interviews 160-1
Douglas-Home, *see* Home
drink 63, 94
drug and alcohol addiction 22
DTI (Department of Trade and Industry) 125
Dubcek, Alexander 80
Dukakis, Michael 89, 90, 104
dynamism 26, 99

Early, Steve 19, 46
economies of scale 88
Eden, Sir Anthony (Lord Avon) 30, 47, 53, 69
Edinburgh, Duke of 36
Edison, Thomas Alva 17, 78
editors 14, 27, 37, 45, 129
education 65, 85
Education Reform Act (1988) 88
Edward VIII, King 120
  *see also* Wales (Edward), Prince of
Edward, Prince 36
Edwardes, Sir Michael 159
Eisenhower, Dwight D 27, 28, 29, 31, 54, 72
elections, *see* by-elections; Europe; General Elections; local government elections
electronics 27, 43, 117
élites 96
  governing 62, 66, 96
  industrial 67
  influence 95
  power 13, 95, 127, 128
Elizabeth I, Queen 11
Elizabeth II, Queen 35, 36, 72, 80
Elizabeth of York 9
ENG (electronic news gathering) 154, 158
Epstein, Brian 93
Europe 120, 125, 164, 165, 166
  Conservatives outfought in elections 137-8
*Evening News* 15
*Evening Standard* 140
Expressionism 26
extended interviews 163-9
eyes 33, 43-4, 58, 103
  eye-lock 50

'f-word' 166
face
  expression 132
  features 60
  hair 46
*Face, The* 54
failed campaigns 183

fairness 86, 138
Falklands 66, 154, 169
  Task force 133, 134
family 70-1
  *see also* royal family
Family Credit Scheme 88
fashions 52, 124
FBI (Federal Bureau of Investigation) 23, 24
federalism 166
feedback 137, 148
films 11, 21, 22, 24, 26, 48, 111-12
  'American values' 22, 85
  reinforcing stories of German atrocities 20
  *Royal Family* 35-6
*Financial Times* 111
first impressions 39-80
first-past-the-post voting system 89
Fisher, Admiral 142
fitness and health 46-8
Flanagan, Bud 30
Fleming, Ian 96
Fletcher, Winston 177
Fonda, Henry 123
Foot, Michael 45, 54
Forbes, Bryan 109, 111
Ford, Gerald 47, 90, 136, 137, 171
foreign clients 145
free speech 151, 182, 183
'Freedom and Fairness' campaign (1986) 111
Freud, Sigmund 17, 56
friends 71
Friese-Greene, William 19
Frost, David 113, 150, 165
Fry, Christopher 173
functional benefit 87

Gable, Clark 21
gaffes 100
Gaitskell, Hugh 31, 99, 173
Galbraith, J K 107
Gallup 29, 97
Garvin, J L 142
gangsters 22, 23, 24
Garbo, Greta 20
Garrett, James 109
Gatorade 124
Gaulle, Charles de 78, 170
gaze behaviour 50
General Elections 74-5, 138
  (1945) 149
  (1950) 30
  (1951) 97, 149
  (1959) 31, 92, 99
  (1964) 99, 100
  (1970) 116, 142, 151, 152
  (1979) 97, 98, 116
  (1987) 65, 99, 106, 113, 143
General Motors 144

General Strike (1926) 18, 130
George III, King 35
George V, King 36
George VI, King 19
Gerasimov, Gennadi 136
Gilmore, Fiona 120, 121
Gladstone, William Ewart 15
glasses, *see* spectacles; sunglasses
GLC (Greater London Council) 111
globalization 93
Goebbels, (Paul) Josef 24-7, 116
Goldwater, Barry 100, 101, 102
Goldwyn, Samuel 21
Gorbachev, Mikhail S 47, 54, 136, 137, 172
Gorbachev, Raisa M 71
governing élite 62, 66, 96
Graham, Billy 41, 116, 118
gramophone records 25
Grant, Cary 22, 52
Great Bible 10
Greer, Ian 147
Griffith, David Wark 20
grooming 51, 57-8, 94-5
Gropius, Walter 119
Gulf War 54, 68, 142, 145
Gulliver, James 65
Gummer, Peter 40, 105

Hagerty, James 72
Haines, Joe 142, 173
hair 53, 55
    dyed 45, 94
    styles 45-6, 58
Haldeman, H R 33
Hall, Tony 154
Halpern, Sir Ralph 145
Hanson 145
Hanvey, John 75
Hardie, Keir 53
Harmsworth, Alfred Charles, *see* Northcliffe
Harmsworth, Harold, *see* Rothermere
Harris, 'Bumper' 122
Harris Research 75
Harrison, William Henry 63
Hart, David 106
hats 53, 56
Hatton, Derek 112
Hawke, Bob 115
headlines 13, 102, 113, 139, 149, 168
health 66, 75
    fitness and 46-8, 93
Hearst, William Randolph 129
Heath, Edward 30, 47, 63, 73, 102, 116, 151

helped by distinguished war record 66
packaging of 108-10
Hegarty, John 76
Henry VII (Tudor), King 9, 10, 119
Henry VIII, King 10, 11
Heren, Louis 129
Heseltine, Michael 71, 140
Heseltine, William 36
Hewitt, Patricia 110
Hill, Lord 151
Hitler, Adolf 24, 25-6, 51, 119
hobbies 72-3
Holbein (The Younger), Hans 10
Hollywood 30, 59, 67, 70, 122
    films 20, 21, 22-3, 24, 85, 111
    lessons from 42-3
Home, Sir Alec Douglas-Home, Lord 69, 90, 102, 172
homosexuality 22, 69, 97
Hoover, Herbert 19, 24, 61, 66
Hoover, John Edgar 23, 129
Horton, Willie 104
Howe, Sir Geoffrey, and Lady 70
Hudson, Hugh 111
Hughes, Howard 22
Hume, David 177
humour
    image-making 173-5
    sense of 135, 136, 173, 174
Humphrey, Hubert 67
Hurd, Douglas 65
hype 20, 21, 112

ICI (Imperial Chemical Industries) 52
illness 47
    *see also* health
image-making scams 155
impressions
    dressing 52-6
    employee 94
    first 39-80
*In Search of Excellence* (Peters and Waterman) 94
independent television 30, 35
    *see also* ITN
individuality 52, 54, 56, 58, 76
influencers 143
informality 51, 54
Ingham, Sir Bernard 73, 76, 143, 156, 159, 163, 165, 174

advice and closeness to Thatcher 133-4, 159, 160, 166-7, 171, 172
own personality, and media's perception of Thatcher 134
institutions 96-7
intellect 26, 42, 65, 181
interviews 50, 60, 156
    first, with a public figure 13
    patronizing 158
    training for 49
    types of 156-72
    *see also* television interviews
issues 82, 85, 138, 155, 173
    minor 166
    religious 66, 67-8
ITN (Independent Television News) 140, 150, 154, 155

Jackson, Andrew ('Old Hickory') 65-6
Jagger, Mick 62, 64, 93
Jamieson, Kathleen Hall 67
Jay, Peter 70
Jefferson, Thomas 67, 79
Jews 26, 67, 129
John Birch Society 123
Johnson, Lyndon Baines 72, 100, 101, 102, 129
    'Great Society' crusade 99
    nefarious activities of brother 70
    voice coaching 59
    war record 66
    wealth 69
Johnson, Sam 70
Johnson & Johnson 144
Jones, Sir John Harvey 45, 52
Jones, Michael 41, 79, 133-4
Joseph, Sir Keith 78
journalists 55, 63, 157-8, 170, 177
    briefers and 133, 135, 137
    friendly 170
    harassed 113
    lazy 136
    lobby 111, 134, 143
    muck-raking, anti-trust 144
    posher media 71
    Press Corps pool 159
    professional 'shits' 149
    revolution in broadcast journalism 150-2
    self-confident 163
    studying the interests of 172
    tabloid 13-14
Junor, Sir John 142
jury consultants 43

Kamen, Michael 112
Kaufman, Gerald 142
Kefauver, Estes 27
Kennedy, John Fitzgerald
  27, 47, 67, 90, 95, 100
  'Camelot' image 71
  dress 53
  family 70, 105
  hairstyle 45
  health 47, 66, 80
  news conferences 130,
    170
  Nixon *versus* 31-5, 69
  showbiz endorsement 123
  wearing of glasses 44
  youthful energy and
    panache 99
Kennedy, Edward (Teddy)
  70, 105
Kennedy, Jackie
  (Jacqueline) 70
Kennedy, Nigel 62
Kennedy, Robert (Bobby)
  70
Kerpel, Tony 137, 138
Khrushchev, Nikita 43, 74,
  80
King, Martin Luther 78
Kinnock, Neil 52, 64, 89, 91,
  105, 120
  atheistic tendencies
    obfuscated 67-8
  CND membership lapsed
    76
  grooming 57
  hairstyle 46
  intellect 65
  *Kinnock the movie* 110-13
  popularity 75
  posture when speaking 59
  press attitude to 110-11
  set-piece television
    interviews 141
  wearing of 'regimental-
    style' ties 56
Kipling, Rudyard 76, 130,
  136
knocking copy 100, 102, 105
Kroc, Ray 78
Ku Klux Klan 101
Kurland, Philip 45

Labour party 90-1, 95, 98,
  100, 118, 139
  European Parliament
    elections (1989) 137
  language and labels 175-6
  leaks 143
  left-wing members 53, 63,
    111
  policy review process 180
  popularity 75
  *see also* Attlee; Callaghan;
    Foot; Gaitskell;
    Kinnock; Wilson (H)

lack of gravitas 54, 174-6
lager louts 93
language
  and labels 175
  persuasive 86
  *see also* body language
'latitude of acceptance'
  theory 146
law enforcement 22
Lawson, Sir Christopher
  115, 120
Lawson, Nigel 140
leaders 16
  personality 84, 110, 114,
    134, 153, 154; and
  choosing an image 95
  *see also under individual
    names*
leaks 142-3, 151, 173
Le Bon, G 24
Le Carré, John 96
Lee, Ivy L 16, 128, 143
left-wing politicians 53, 64,
  111, 178
  American 79-80
Lenin, Vladimir Ilyich 19
Liberal party 90
lies 26, 40, 101
  as exaggeration,
    calculated omission and
    synthetic
  emotion 180
  organized 16-17
  super-liars 48-51
Lilley, Peter 158
Lincoln, Abraham 12, 22,
  95, 179
line extensions 89, 90-1, 122
Lippman, Walter 178
Lloyd George, David 15, 26,
  52, 59
Lloyds Bank 121
lobby 14, 111, 128, 138, 143,
  147-8
local government elections
  82, 137, 138, 139
'log cabin' strategy 62-3
logos 96, 111, 120, 177
Lotus Computers 68
loudspeakers 25
Lucozade 93
Lufthansa 94

Maastricht 137
MacDonald, Ramsay 29, 130
McGinnis, Joe 103
Machiavelli, Niccolò 103
McKenzie, Kelvin 77
Macleod, Iain 90, 102
McLuhan, Marshall 131,
  132
Macmillan, Harold (Lord
  Stockton) 25, 28, 35, 47,
  66, 98, 142, 150
  coached in acting 30

dress 54
penchant for ducal living
  63
'Supermac' 31, 74
wealth 69
Madison, James 79
magazines 15, 17
Magee, John Gillespie 175
Major, John 30, 48, 64, 91,
  105, 137, 173
  accent 62
  clothes 54; and
    appearance 55
  doorstep interviews 159
  education 65
  'honest John' image 55
  'nasal resonance' speech
    60
  popularity 75
  sporting image 72, 95
make-up 32, 33, 42, 48, 58,
  164
makeover process 20-1, 30
'man of the people' image
  62
managers
  crisis 128, 144-5
  news 127-9
  party 14
Mandela, Winnie 71
Mandelson, Peter 99, 110,
  180
Mannes, Marya 81
market research 82-6, 180
marketing 81-125, 180, 181
  direct 83, 114-16
  personality 108-14
Mars 78, 115
Marshall, Sir Colin 94
Marx, Karl 83
mass meetings 25, 116, 117
media 128, 146, 170, 181
  access to 156
  assessing reaction of 170
  Bernstein/Woodward
    inspired 63
  bias of 149
  briefers and 133-42
  hot and cool 131-3
  image-making scams and
    155
  influencing 143
  lobbyists 143-6
  monitoring 150, 162
  'politically correct' line on
    ageism 47
  posher 72
  relationships with 133,
    150
  right kind of coverage
    152
  *see also* radio; newspapers;
    television
Mehrabian, Professor 41
*Mein Kampf* 26

Mencken, H L 149
Meyer, Sir Anthony 137, 141, 164
MI5/MI6 142
microphones 18, 25, 44, 56
Militant 111
military intelligence 96
Mill, John Stuart 177
Millar, Sir Ronnie 109, 173, 174
Mille, Cecil B de 20
Miller, Jonathan 131
*Minder* 62
minders 128, 149-56, 159-60, 162, 164, 167
Ministry of Defence 133, 154
Mitchell, Leslie 30
'mockney' 62
Mondale, Walter 136, 137
Monopolies Commission 148
Monroe, Marilyn 21
Montgomery, Field Marshal Bernard Law 51, 77
Moore, Mary Tyler 123
Moran, Lord 47
More, Sir Thomas 9
MORI 112
Morita, Akio 78
*Morning Star* 162
Morris, Desmond 49, 50, 58
Morrison, Peter 173
muscle relaxation exercises 60
music 112, 117, 118
Mussolini, Benito 24, 25, 51, 59, 119

Nader, Ralph 144
Nadir, Asil 92, 93
Napoleon I, Emperor of France 51, 129
Napoleon III, Emperor of France 46
national curriculum 88
National Front 143
*National Review* 173
National Socialism, *see* Nazi Germany
National Trust 124
National Westminster Bank 94, 121
NATO 113
Naughtie, James 168, 169
Nazi Germany 24-7
NBC (National Broadcasting Company) 18, 19, 136, 144
negroes 67
neologisms 17
nepotism 70
'new broom' mentality 121
New Deal 19, 99
new products 91-2

*New Statesman* 99
*New York Herald* 12
*New York Morning Journal* 129
*New York Post* 27
*New York Times* 19, 129
*New York Tribune* 13
*New York World* 129
news
  broadcasts 130, 162
  conferences 169-71
  editors 154
  gathering 131
  management 21, 23, 127-76
  shaping 143-9
  television editors and 37
*News of the World* 12, 98
newscasters 50
newspapers 11-12, 18, 26-7, 36, 63, 70, 130
  hegemony over communications 17
  hostile 129
  institutionalized 149
  invention with biggest effect on 16
  new popular 15
  'profile' interviews 157-8
  support for Labour 151
  tabloid 13, 71, 180
  transcript interviews 157
  *see also under individual titles*
newsreels 19, 20, 26
NHS (National Health Service) 85, 100
Nixon, Don 70
Nixon, Richard Milhous 27-8, 36, 44, 67, 72, 79
  cronies 71
  Dimbleby's satirical comments on 151
  family 70
  Kennedy *versus* 31-5, 69
  Khrushchev's description of 43
  news conferences 170
  pardon after Watergate 90
  shifty image 34
  showbiz endorsement 123
  TV Specials (1968) 103
'non-attack' attack formula 106
nonverbal leakage 49
Noonan, Peggy 80, 174-5
Norfolk, Duke of 35, 68
Northcliffe, Lord 11, 15, 129
NUM (National Union of Mineworkers) 145

obesity 46
*Observer, The* 15, 98, 142

Ogilvy, David 94, 107
Oldfield, Sir Maurice 96
Olney knot 56
one-liners, *see* ad libs; slogans
opinion polls 34, 89, 138, 140, 164, 165-6
  privately-commissioned 143
  *see also* market research
O'Sullivan, John 173
'outing' campaigns 45
outside broadcasts 29, 35, 153
Oval office 18-19
Owen, Dr David 112

Packard, Vance 107
*Pall Mall Gazette* 13
Parkinson, Cecil 108
Parliamentary lobbyists, *see* lobby
Patten, Chris 62
Patton, General George 51
Peel, Sir Robert 61
'people meter' method 112, 180-1
performance 132, 140, 156, 166
Perrier crisis 144
personal endorsements 122
personality
  brand 94-5
  choices expressing 54-5
  clothes and 52
  criminal 46
  cult of 112
  hairstyles and 45
  illusory 181
  influence of 73-80
  leaders 84, 110, 114, 134, 153, 154
  Machiavellian 74
  marketing 108-14
  'reading', from faces 43
  ties and 56
Peters, Michael 119
pets 28, 72
phone-in interviews 169
photographers 128, 182
photo-opportunities 63, 72, 139, 152-6
physical appearance 33-4, 39, 40-58, 95, 132, 181
Pigs, Bay of 129
Pincus, Charlie 44
pitch and resonance 59-60
'placing' people 41-2
police 22, 24, 96-7
political advertising 83, 85, 103, 177, 180-1
  attack 105
  contribution to political process 114
  election 98-9, 102, 120, 152

negative 82, 100, 104-6
picture research 97-8
poll tax 138
terrorists 128
why it works 106-8
political communication 18,
    24, 85, 86, 113, 135
    essential with voters 111
    most vital target 153
    speeches a mainstay of
    172
    strategies 92, 117, 138
poll tax 86, 138-9, 140, 176,
    178
polls, *see* opinion polls
pollsters 29, 34, 139
popularity 75, 84
Porter, Tom 58
positioning 86-97, 122, 177
*Post, The* 34
posture 59, 163
Powell, Sir Charles 110
Powell, Chris 110
Powell, Enoch 54, 78
power élite 13, 95, 127, 128
PR (public relations) 12, 17,
    51, 76, 128, 144
    and business mega-bids
    145-7
    police 97
    royal family 36, 156
preparation 35, 160, 162-8
press 23, 36, 70, 141, 154
    agents 16, 20, 183
    anti-Labour 149
    barons 129, 130
    censorship 13
    corps 46
    power of 11-13
    relations with 111
    releases 23
    Tory 110, 149, 150
    *see also* newspapers
Press Association 12
pressure groups 127, 144,
    155
privatization 85
product placement 124
Profumo, John 30, 35
pronunciation 61-2
propaganda 10, 15, 24, 26,
    99
props 41, 43, 51-2
Proust, Marcel 43
Prudential 121
psephologists 75, 138
psychology 24, 26, 57, 87
public speakers 24, 50, 172
publicity 21, 22, 23, 67
    free 177
Pulitzer, J 129
Purvis, Stewart 154

Quant, Mary 119
Quayle, Dan 90

radio 16, 17-19, 24, 61, 132,
    139
    wartime, German 25, 26
Raft, George 23
rallies 173
    conferences and 116-18
Rambova, Natacha 21
Rayban 124
Reagan, Jack 79
Reagan, Nancy 71
Reagan, Ronald 72, 83, 92,
    103, 159, 179
    birthplace image 63
    Bush's line extension to
    89
    colour choice 58
    films 48, 79, 85, 111
    humour 174-5
    Labour defence policy
    intervention 113
    meetings with Gorbachev
    54, 137, 172
    news conferences 170,
    171
    'non-attack' attack
    formula 106
    personality 84
    publicity, through Irish
    ancestors 67
    voice 59, 61·
    wearing of glasses 44
    wrongly accused of
    dyeing hair 45
received pronunciation 61
Reece, Sir Gordon 109,
    144-5, 154, 155
    advice to Thatcher 153;
    poll tax 178; voice
    coaching 60; wearing hats
    on television 57
Reeves, Rosser 28-9
Reform Acts
    (1832) 11
    (1867) 12, 14
'regimental' ties 56
regional accent 61
rehearsals 162-4, 169, 170
Reiss, Charles 140
Reith, Sir John 18, 35·
religion 66, 67-8
reporters 23, 103, 140, 153,
    160, 161-2
    agency 12
    investigative 13-16
    leakers ingratiating
    themselves with 143
    *see also* journalists
research
    advisers 180
    effect of 82-6
    picture 98
    values 85
resonance 59-60
rhinoplasty 44
Richard III, King 9, 10

Ridley, Nicholas 148
Riefenstahl, Leni 25
Riesman, David 83, 84
robber barons 16, 144
Rockefeller, John D 16-17
Rockefeller, Nelson A 136
Rogers, Ted 27-8, 32, 33, 34
Roman Catholic Church 22,
    77, 96
Roosevelt, Eleanor 71
Roosevelt, Franklin Delano
    18, 44, 72, 79, 130, 149,
    174
    fireside chats 18, 150
    first television address 27
    paralysis 46
    showbiz endorsement 123
Rothermere, Lord 15, 129,
    130
royal family 155-6
Russell, William Howard 13

Saatchi & Saatchi 102, 113
*St Louis Dispatch* 34
Salinger, Pierre 34, 71, 123,
    130, 170
*Salisbury* (newspaper) 15
Salmon, John 105
Sands, Bobby 128
SAS (Special Air Service) 96
Sassoon, Vidal 119
Savundra, Emil 150
SCA (Shadow
    Communications
    Agency) 110, 111
scandal 70, 71, 90, 144, 157
    control of 20, 21-2
Scarfe, Gerald 152
Scargill, Arthur 167
Schlesinger, Arthur 127
Scottish Nationalists 123
Scott, Randolph 22
SDP (Social Democratic
    Party) 115, 177
Second World War 85
sense of humour 135, 136,
    173, 174
Shakespeare, William 9
Shaw, George Bernard 62
Shea, Michael 145, 183
shoes 56
showbiz endorsements
    123-4
signals
    class 63
    visual 41
Singapore Airlines 94
single-mindedness 76, 78,
    135
SIS (Secret Intelligence
    Service) 96
slanging matches 158-9, 160
Sloan, Alfred P 119
'Sloane Rangers' 54
slogans 28-9, 65, 92, 102,
    117, 177

aimed at the lowest
  intellect 26
forged 149
smears 26, 101, 137
Smith, Al 61, 66, 67, 149
Smith, Chris 68
Smith, Pete 21
SmithKline Beecham 93
smoking 63, 94, 145-6, 182,
  183
Snow, Peter 167-8
Social Charter 166
Social Security Act (1986) 88
socialism 110, 120
  democratic 90
  principles 76
Sorensen, Theodore 67
sound-bites 130-1, 159, 160,
  180
  pre-recorded 161-2
Speakes, Larry 136, 137,
  169, 170, 172
spectacles 44, 55, 57, 58
speech 103
  free 151, 182, 183
  London 60, 62
  patterns 175
speech therapy 60
speeches 85, 100, 111,
  131-2, 137, 172-6
  Nazi propaganda 25, 26
  political careers smashed
    by 78
  researched using 'people
    meter' method 112,
    178-9
speechwriters 172, 174
Speer, Albert 25
Spillane, Mary 57, 58
spin doctoring 136-42, 170
*Sportsnight with Coleman* 109
stage-management 25, 116
Stalin, Joseph 51, 80
Stanford Research Institute
  83
status-displays 50-1
Stead, W T 13-14
Steel, Sir David 112
Sternberg, Josef von 20
Stevenson, Adlai 27, 28, 66
Steward, George 130
Stewart, James (Jimmy) 22
Stiller, Mauritz 20
Stock, Francine 158
Strathclyde University 145
style 52, 55, 56, 63, 120
subliminal ideas 121
*Sun* 77, 139
*Sunday Express* 27, 142
*Sunday Pictorial* 98
*Sunday Telegraph* 172
*Sunday Times, The* 41, 55, 79,
  112, 134
super-liars 48-51
super stare 160

Superbowl 124
'Supermac', see Macmillan
surgery 44-5
'Svengalis' 20
swastika 25
symbols 9, 86, 119, 120-1
  *see also* logos

Takeover Panel 105
takeovers 11, 65
target groups 83, 98, 112,
  116
'target teams' 154
taste 63
Tebbit, Norman 106
technology 10, 132, 153,
  154
Teeter, Robert 103
teeth 44-5
television 27-37, 75, 121,
  168, 174, 179
  advent of 34, 41, 49
  comments on
    performance 55
  executives, and
    impartiality 149
  firsts 130
  generation 175
  households owning 131
  live 137
  manners 158-9
  messages 132-3
  news 140, 167
  qualities most likely to be
    revealed by 74
  reporters 21
  series 24
  sound-bites 130-1, 159,
    160, 161-2, 180
  trial by 150
  'walls' 117
  *see also* ABC; BBC; CBS;
    ITN; NBC
television interviews 56,
  139, 150, 157-8
  pre-recorded 'bites' 160-2
  set-piece 142
terrorism 127, 142
Thatcher, Carol 57, 70
Thatcher, Denis 70
Thatcher, Margaret 18, 41,
  48, 63, 83, 180
  against attack advertising
    105
  applauded by eastern
    European leaders 80
  backbench rumours of
    performance 140
  *bon mots* 172
  doorstep interviews 159,
    160
  doubts over leadership
    139
  first conference speech
    (1975) 173

fitness 47
grooming 56
individuality 76
Ingham and 133-4, 159,
  166-7, 171, 172
leadership challenge 138,
  140, 165
leaky Cabinet 143
one-liners 30
personality 153
phone-in frustration over
  *Belgrano* 169
poll tax and downfall 86
popularity 75, 84, 112
portrayed as anti-EC 164
sense of humour 173
speculation about future
  164
Stakhanovite image 72
traditional challenger
  strategy 90
voice 60, 61
wealth 69
Thatcher, Mark 71
Thatcherism 120
Thomas, Harvey 41, 116,
  117, 118
'Thursday Team' 109-10
ties 56
Tilden, Bill 68
*Time* magazine 71
*Times, The* 12, 15, 36, 65,
  141, 142
  Berlin correspondents'
    dispatches censored 129
  Crimean War dispatches
    13
  Duke of Norfolk's
    'blasphemy' letter 68
*Tit-Bits* 15
tobacco 21, 146, 183
Tory party, *see* Conservative
  party
trade unions 16, 91, 106,
  145
Transport House 150
Truman, Harry S 79
Tucker, Geoffrey 108, 109,
  116
TV-AM 113
Twain, Mark 177

United States
  clothes/headgear as
    politicians' props 51
  'competence and caring'
    strategy 91
  conference techniques
    117
  Conservatives' study of
    impact of television 30
  homosexual congressmen
    68
  importance of the tie 56
  'jury consultants' 42

'liberalism' a dirty word
    166
marketing techniques 81
Nazi propaganda to 26
number of households
    owning a television 131
slogans 28
*see also* Bush; Carter;
    Eisenhower; Ford;
    Harrison; Hoover;
    Johnson (LB); Kennedy
    (JF); Lincoln; Nixon;
    Reagan; Roosevelt;
    Truman; Van Buren;
    Wilson (W)
USP (unique selling
    proposition) 29

Valentino, Rudolph 21
values
    all-American 22-3
    core 88, 89, 91
    deeply held 83
    family 85
    production 114
    traditional 84
Van Buren, Martin 62, 63
van der Rohe, Mies 119, 136
van Dyke, Dick 123
Vatican 96, 149
verbal deception 49
verbiage 176
'Vicky' 30
Victoria, Queen 15, 19, 51,
    122
video technology 152, 154
visual signals 41
voice 43, 58-62, 109
voters 12, 74, 181
    average 75, 182
    choices 84, 114
    first-time 124

floating 112, 113, 146
good communications
    with 111
Labour 84

Wagner, Richard 25
Wakeham, John 80
Waldegrave, William 62,
    168
Walden, Brian 167
Wales, Charles, Prince of
    36, 49, 60, 119
Wales, Diana, Princess of
    37, 71, 80, 156
Wales, Edward (VIII),
    Prince of 52
walkabouts 109, 152, 156
Wall, Christine 72
Wall Street 67
*Wall Street Journal* 56
WAM (Week Ahead
    Meeting) 165
Wandsworth 138, 139
war records 65-6, 85
Washington Press Club 80
Watergate 77, 90
Watson, Thomas J 78
Weldon, Huw 152
Welles, Orson 123
Werwick, Maynard 10
whips' office 14, 68
White, Michael 54, 153
White, Theodore 32, 85
*Who's Who* 65
Wigg, George 142
Wight, Robin 89
wigs 45
Wilde, Oscar 39
Williams, Marcia (Lady
    Falkender) 156, 173
Williams, Pete 68
Wilson, Bill 32, 34, 67

Wilson, Sir Harold (Lord
    Wilson of Rievaulx)
    90, 109-10, 150, 156, 172
    admiration of Kennedy
        99
    cronies and scandal 71
    Machiavellian personality
        74
    the 'common touch' 63
    humour 173
    income from writing 69
    one liners 30
    policy on leaking 142
    popularity 75
    'thoughtful pipe' image
        52
    Tory broadcast abuse of
        102
Wilson, John King 54
Wilson, Kemmons 78
Wilson, Woodrow 20, 46
'Winter of Discontent' 91
Wirthlin, Richard 78, 84,
    85, 86, 103
*Wogan* 166
Wolfe, Tom 93
words
    dirty 166
    power 129-30
    primacy of image over 31
    spoken 25
wordsmiths 128, 172-5
Wrigley, Philip K 108
Wyatt, Woodrow 98, 133

Yeltsin, Boris N 80
Young, Brigham 13
Young, David 148

*Zinoviev letter 149*
*Zola, Emile 46*